Sociology Projects

Sociology Projects

A Students' Guide

David Barrat and Tony Cole

First published in 1991
by Routledge
11 New Fetter Lane, London EC4P 4EE

Printed in Great Britain by
Richard Clay (The Chaucer Press) Ltd.
Bungay, Suffolk

British Library Cataloguing in Publication Data
Barrat, David
  Sociology projects : a students' guide.
  1. Sociology
  I. Title   II. Cole, Tony
  301

ISBN 0–415–04863–X

Contents

Foreword

The publication of this book is an occasion of particular satisfaction to me, let alone its authors. Having been associated with A level Sociology almost since its inception in 1966, I have long been aware of the contradiction between the enquiring and challenging nature of the discipline itself and the increasingly ponderous and uninspiring rut into which it has sunk under the stultifying influence of the traditional A level syllabus and examination. Much of the teaching has been so good and so inventive that it has been an even greater sadness that the examination has remained remorselessly traditional, being based on the principle that the best way to assess students' achievements is to sit them down in silence, probably on a hot day, and to require them to write four essays in three hours in response to titles that they have seen only a few minutes earlier.

In the first twenty-five years of A level Sociology, there has been only one serious exception to this uniformity - the Mode 3 A level syllabus, developed at Loughton College and approved by the Associated Examining Board, which required that students should carry out a sociological enquiry. I was appointed Moderator for this syllabus in 1979 and learned in the next few years what A level Sociology could be like and what standards students could reach when they were well taught by skilled teachers working with an imaginative syllabus which enabled students to 'do sociology' as well as to read about it. David Barrat and Tony Cole, the authors of this book, were members of the team who developed and taught that unique syllabus.

And yet the research-based project (though under the more distinguished title of 'dissertation' or 'thesis') has long been the main method of assessing a student's achievement in the post-A level stages of education. First degrees usually include a thesis, master's degrees are mostly based on research, and Ph.Ds are awarded entirely on the basis of the student's ability to complete original research under supervision.

Though there was experience of project work at 14-16, especially in CSE Mode 3 syllabuses, the important breakthrough came with the introduction of the GCSE and its emphasis on assessing what students 'know, understand and can do'. With the move to a skills based curriculum at 14-16, A level had to follow. Within a couple of years, the AEB had introduced a project option in their syllabus, the London Board (ULSEB) offered an AS level syllabus with 50% of the assessment being based

Foreword

on a compulsory enquiry, and both the Oxford and Cambridge Boards revised their syllabuses to include an element of research-based coursework. At the time of writing, the die appears finally to have been cast, with the SEAC's Draft Principles for A and AS level advocating that all assessment schemes should include up to 40% for coursework. At last then, students will be able to experience for themselves the challenge and the excitement of social research, and will be rewarded for doing it well.

But they will need guidance, ideas and advice. No-one is better equipped to provide this guidance, through their experience and expertise, than the authors of this book.

The book is, essentially, a distillation of what David Barrat and Tony Cole learned during the period of their Mode 3 syllabus at Loughton. They understand what it is that A level and other beginning students need to know about sociological research, and, perhaps as important, what they do **not** need to know. They appreciate the practical limitations of time, money, libraries and other resources within which the student operates, whether at school or at college. They have no theoretical or methodological axe to grind. They are familiar with the requirements and assessment objectives of the syllabus (not least because Tony Cole has been involved in developing at least two of them). Both have published successful A level texts before (Barrat 1986, Cole 1986) and they know the level of writing and of sophistication that is appropriate. They know the possibilities and the pitfalls, whether practical, ethical or theoretical, of student research and they guide the reader through them.

A particular characteristic of this book, and one which is likely to distinguish it from many of its competitors, is its emphasis on how almost anything can be used as data in a sociological enquiry. The ideas and advice on how documents, statistics, artefacts and other human creations can be given sociological significance and meaning are unusual and stimulating. 'You don't have to do a survey', they say, and students will be well advised to heed this advice.

Students who use this book will not only be able to do research as part of their A level assessment - they will enjoy doing it.

Pat McNeill

Introduction

The aim of this book is to give a practical and theoretical guide to doing a sociological research enquiry. It is designed for students on A level, AS level, Access and other courses in sociology where some kind of enquiry or research study is involved. Students in higher education may also find it useful, especially if they have not done any sociological research before.

The background to the book is twofold: biographical and historical. The first concerns our experience as teachers on a unique Mode 3 course work assessed A level syllabus at Loughton College which ran from 1978 to 1985. Many of our observations and examples come from teaching on this syllabus. The second refers to the recent growth in the number of syllabuses offering or requiring some kind of assessed student enquiry. The main ones, as we write this book, are the AEB (Associated Examining Board) A level (664) and the London AS level (585).

In addition to this, the Oxford and Cambridge Boards have carried out syllabus revisions - one of the authors was involved in each of these revisions - though the future of all social science A and AS levels is currently the subject of much discussion. One of us has been invited to join a working party of all the GCE examining boards looking at this provision. Pressures for change have been coming from many sources: centres, teachers and candidates; the Department of Education and Science;

the Schools Examinations and Assessment Council (SEAC); the National Curriculum Council.

Further comment on these last two organisations is appropriate here. Firstly we should note that in its documents on the assessment of A level in Sociology, SEAC argues for the principle that course work and/or personal investigation be part of this assessment. From 1994, SEAC will have the power to impose its guidelines of good practice on the examining boards and their syllabuses.

Secondly, there is the National Curriculum Council (NCC) policy on core skills for 16-19 year olds. Six such skills are identified: communication; problem solving; personal skills; numeracy; information technology; modern language competence. We believe that sociology is well placed to meet the first four or five of these, though the skills are more readily incorporated into syllabuses with personal study/coursework assessment.

While fully supporting the trend towards some sort of sociological research enquiry, we do recognise that there are some problems in this. Nonetheless it does seem that the future at A level is the enquiry and we hope that this book makes it a lot easier to deal with.

In addition to GCE A and AS level, there are a wide range of courses, such as BTEC National, Access, first year undergraduate and so on where a sociological enquiry is involved and where this book can provide guidance.

Because there are so many existing or developing Sociology syllabuses where some kind of project is involved, it is not appropriate or practical to give details of them all. A copy of your syllabus should be available from your college or school, or directly from the examination board. However, a few general comments about the type of enquiry we are concerned with are called for:

Scale

We are assuming an enquiry that could be completed in one term, though it may well take longer, and which is likely to be around 3,000-5,000 words long.

Assessment objectives

Though each course or syllabus will have its own specific requirements, it is likely that marks will be awarded for a mixture of qualities demonstrated:

- choice, aims and explanation of research topic;
- methods chosen, with justification given;
- findings;
- interpretation;
- evaluation and conclusion.

All these issues will be addressed in this book. One particular point we are assuming is that it is very likely that you'll be assessed on **how** you carried out your enquiry and not on the findings alone.

Research methods

The chapters of this book explore the various merits, and otherwise, of gathering data yourself (primary research) and using material that already exists (secondary research). This distinction is explored more fully on pages 41-43. Some syllabuses view these with equal acceptance; others may not. You need to be clear on this. Where there is no specific requirement, it's our view that, as far as possible, you should use both. Secondary data, even if only existing sociological literature, can provide ideas, theories and suggestions for methods and lines of enquiry. Primary research, by which we don't just mean interviews, can give a sense of personal involvement to your enquiry and make it more specifically yours. These ideas are developed more fully later.

The place of the enquiry on the syllabus

Our experience with Mode 3 A level sociology and our involvement with sociology at various levels over many years suggest that a research enquiry can make a very positive contribution to teaching and learning sociology. We would like to make a few observations on this under two general headings:

Changing the sociology game

One of the main and obvious influences of the syllabuses that incorporate a student enquiry is that less time has to be devoted to the imparting of knowledge. More class and private study time can be student-directed with the tutor's role becoming that of a consultant, not just a knowledge giver. Individual tutorials about the enquiry can also improve the level of understanding and interaction between the student and tutor.

One of the things we particularly enjoyed about teaching on a Mode 3 syllabus was how much we were able to learn from the ideas and topic choices of our students. Their questions often forced us to think about new issues and problems, or to see old issues in a new light.

In short, these courses can promote the development and use of that crucial but elusive quality: the sociological imagination.

Another important consideration is that, as a student-directed activity, project work is particularly appropriate for open-learning and evening classes. Here, although attendance may be irregular, the students can continue their studies despite any loss of class contact. At Loughton, we employed our Mode 3 enquiry based scheme with all classes, including part time, one year, day and evening classes.

Assessing a wider range of abilities

Over the years, many sociology teachers have argued that there is at least a potential contradiction between the requirements of conventional Mode 1 examinations and the understanding of sociology that they are hoping their students will acquire. They argued that conventional exams put a premium on knowledge particularly on the research findings of professional sociologists as summarised in well known text books. They contrasted this with a view of sociology as being about questions as well as answers and emphasised the importance of an understanding of how sociological knowledge is produced.

It was this stress upon acquiring understanding through doing, by trying to gather evidence or apply theories and concepts as a way of appreciating the nature of sociology, that lay behind the Mode 3 A level at Loughton College.

Assessing candidates on a wider range of skills or abilities does not only do more justice to the nature of sociological understanding, it has a number of other advantages. The skills acquired, for example, in carrying out a personal study in depth are all relevant and useful in other areas: higher education, outside life, the world of work. The qualities referred to here are those of problem formulating and solving, flexibility of thinking, imagination and enterprise, and the wide range of abilities associated with gathering, interpreting and evaluating data.

We also believe it is fairer to students if they are allowed to demonstrate their sociological ability by means other than the examination essay. To put it another way, the new syllabuses referred to are a more valid measure of sociological understanding because they extend the range of assessment techniques. One of the striking features of our Mode 3 was the very high quality of research projects produced by our one year mature students. They demonstrated both general skills and specific sociological understanding that they would not have been able to demonstrate in the examination room.

Using the book

The book is divided into three sections. Part I is concerned with the choosing and planning of your enquiry, including guidance on the organisation of your work, note-taking, record keeping, library usage and other general skills associated with personal research.

Part II is concerned with sociological research methods. There is a brief, general introduction to some common sociological themes. There then follows a chapter on each of the main research methods that you might use, together with practical and theoretical commentary on their usage. Examples and exercises are used to illustrate the points made.

Part III is concerned with editing, presenting and writing up the data. Using the AEB assessment scheme format, it gives some guidance on how to structure your enquiry to get the best from your earlier work of planning and researching.

Part I

Getting started

Includes

Choosing your enquiry

Planning and doing the enquiry

1

Choosing your enquiry

Choosing what topic or issue to study may well be one of the hardest and is certainly one of the most important parts of doing your research enquiry. It might be hard to choose because you haven't got any ideas or because you have loads of them. Once you have made your choice there are many things which follow on immediately which can give your enquiry a momentum, almost of its own. There are books to be ordered from the library, letters to be sent to organisations, replies to be acted upon, cuttings to be collected or whatever.

Data and ideas should accumulate and, of course, be noted and organised. From the outset, therefore, you could benefit enormously from keeping a log; indeed some syllabuses require one. A log not only assists personal organisation of study but also enables you to record how you came to make your choice of project, the criteria and influences you took into account and so on.

Choosing is important because the topic you pick has a major influence on the level of sustainable interest likely, the ease or difficulty of obtaining data and, in particular, the methods and sources to be used. In choosing your topic or issue, make sure that you consider the scale and focus of the enquiry. If your approach is too broad, it will be too big a topic to research in depth and may well appear like a chapter from a general text book; it will also become quite unmanageable. An example of such an excessively broad topic might

be 'social mobility'. However, a study of social mobility in relation to a particular group or issue would be all right. 'Afro-Caribbean small business as a route to mobility' would be a narrower focus, especially if you looked at one town or business type or if you used secondary data on specific national issues such as race and racism in banking or enterprise schemes. You should consult the Commission for Racial Equality for data or the Directory of British Associations for relevant organisations to consult on this.

Clearly, broad issues may be a context or background to your particular study. Thus, in the example just given, some reference to racism, to immigration or to the different economic and cultural history of West Indians, compared with, say, Asians - who have a history of trading and/or independent peasant production making self employment more likely - could all be useful reference points.

Aims and hypotheses

Focusing on a particular issue rather than a general one is, in effect, about formulating an aim or set of aims to your enquiry. You may be interested in 'race' as a general area and, within that, the way it is dealt with in the mass media. You may then narrow the focus to newspapers, possibly the popular press. One question you may focus upon is the degree to which stories about black people accentuate 'problems' such as poverty, crime, unemployment, as discussed by Hartman and Husband (1974). This could be written as an hypothesis to be tested against a sample of the type of newspaper in question over a given period. A subsidiary hypothesis, or research aim could relate to the voluntary code of conduct adopted by newspaper editors in December 1989. This included a commitment not to refer to a person's race or religion where it is irrelevant to the story. This issue relates to the way some papers referred to black criminal offenders as 'black' but did not describe white offenders as being 'white'. The idea for this subsidiary hypothesis or research question came from the *Hard News* television programme about the press on Channel 4, December 7th 1989, which noted early breaches of this code by one particular newspaper.

How do I choose my enquiry?

Assuming that you have no definite ideas to begin with, there are a number of ways you can begin to generate them.

You could seek inspiration by browsing across the areas or topics that Sociology covers. Look at the syllabus areas on your course, in your text books, at the titles or areas covered by books in the sociology section of the library. Should a given topic or area strike you as particularly interesting, jot it down straight away.

You may, indeed, find a book so interesting that you want to replicate it, ie to do your own research based on the approach of the original authors. So long as you're realistic about the scale of your enquiry there is no reason why you should not do this. Remember, however, the importance of demonstrating your own understanding of the topic, research method and so on.

The next stage is narrowing down the focus. An obvious way to start doing this is to ask yourself why you have chosen, say, crime, as an area of interest. There may be a number of reasons or particular aspects which interest you. You could write these down as a list, noting particularly important key words, or you could seek to generate ideas by some kind of brainstorming note-taking activity, for example a concept tree with key ideas in circles and connecting ideas linked by a line joining these circles (see page 34 for more on this technique).

Group brainstorming often produces more ideas than an individual can, so this is a good classroom activity. Remember that during a brainstorm session, you make a note of every idea that comes up. Don't edit anything until the ideas have dried up.

Another way of focusing down, or indeed choosing a topic in the first place is to write out a list of ideas based on any one of the following: a current political issue; a media event; an interest of yours; an aspect of your experience or social background. With this, you might start with an idea which sounds non-sociological and then seek to develop sociological ways of analysing it. For example, many lines of sociological enquiry can be suggested by seeking to apply key sociological concepts to the issues or activity in question:

- to what extent is the activity differentiated by age, sex, class and ethnicity?
- do the people involved have a particular set of beliefs?
- is power a relevant factor in the analysis?

It's worth emphasising here that, whether or not an approach is sociological, depends on two factors: what is being studied - subject matter; and how it is being studied - perspective. The distinction is important for, as Berger (1966) notes, much of the subject matter of sociology is shared with other disciplines - law, economics, political science and so on. Whilst a full account of the various definitions of the sociological perspective is beyond the scope of this book, we could note briefly two versions of this.

Bilton et al (1981) argue that popular or common sense approaches to human behaviour often stress biological, psychological or moralistic explanations of this behaviour. In particular these authors contrast individualistic explanations with social, ie sociological ones. Individualistic approaches look at personal factors like genetics, personality, moral qualities rather than at social influences like belief systems, social structures and so on.

The second version we cite is that of Berger (1966). He stresses three key features in the sociological perspective. They are: 'debunking motif', 'unrespectability', and 'relativism'. By debunking motif, Berger means that the sociologist needs to adopt a very sceptical stance towards 'official' or 'common sense' definitions of reality, to look for hidden or even deliberately masked structures or social patterns. Unrespectability refers to the requirement to avoid too close a connection to, or immersion in, the respectable world lest this should dull the sociologist's perceptions of poverty, deviance and other problems which 'respectable' or 'nice' views would prefer to ignore or play down. Finally, relativism; this is a hard term to define briefly but is perhaps best understood as a willingness and ability to stand outside one's own social position and to recognise social differences as valid rather than aberrations or incomprehensible deviations from the absolute standards of one's own society or social group.

We refer you to the two texts cited for further illustration of this theme. Also relevant is our later section on social versus sociological problems, especially the reference to Mills (pages 17-18) and the section on sociological and non-sociological literature (especially pages 45-50).

It's not enough to have an idea of what to study or even what particular questions or issues you want to explore. You need to address the question of how you can obtain the information you are interested in. You need to think about the following:

- Is there an available sociological literature on the topic? Your teacher should be able to help here. Alternatively you could browse through references and recommended reading in books.
- Is there a body of literature on the topic of a non-sociological kind? If so, can this be used or adapted for a sociological purpose?
- Are there likely to be organisations that could be sources of data, such as government departments, pressure groups, charities, local clubs etc?
- What are the chances of data from media sources being available and useful?
- Do you have any personal avenues of enquiry that can be followed up, such as some aspect of home/school/college/work life as a basis of contacts and interviews?
- Are there aspects of your own personal experience that are relevant? If so, how can they be used in a sociological manner?

Whatever the answer to these questions, one important piece of advice that will apply to almost any topic is to follow up your initial idea with some reading before you go any further. Detailed dis-

ACTIVITY 1 - WHAT'S IN A TITLE?

This group exercise is designed to help you through some of the issues involved in choosing a topic and then setting out to research it. In groups of two or three select two titles from the list below and then discuss using the questions below.

Project Titles:

'Adoptive Families - are they different?' (by a person who has been adopted).

'Shoplifting among school pupils.'

'Work and family life - a case study: the police officer' (by a police officer's daughter/son).

'The generation gap - a case study of Muslim girls in Britain.'

'Gender and crime. The social process of becoming an official deviant.'

'Does social class affect your educational attainment?'

'Alcohol abuse among the underage.'

'The effects environmental pressure groups have had on public attitudes and ideas.'

'Women's experience at work.'

'How women's magazines portray the ideology of the family.'

'An investigation into racist attitudes.'

'Since 1894, has child abuse increased, is it just more discussed, and how is it handled?'

'A study of two different pressure groups (ANC and RSPCA) and how they work.'

'YTS - a comparison of official views with the experiences and attitudes of trainees.'

'Feminism today and its future prospects.'

'Acid house - a moral panic.'

(This list was selected from actual AS submissions to the London Board plus a few made up by ourselves)

Discussion questions

1. Is the scale of the enquiry too large and ambitious?
2. Is it sufficiently focused onto a particular topic or question?
3. Are there legal or ethical obstacles to the topic or the methods likely to be used?
4. Is there likely to be a high level of personal involvement?
5. If so, will this be a bonus or a problem?
6. Is the topic usually covered in sociological literature?
7. If not, how could it be approached sociologically?
8. What concepts or ideas are suggested by the title?
9. How could they be converted into research questions?
10. What methods or sources of data could be used? (eg observation, interviews, questionnaires, media analysis, organisational sources, books etc).

cussion on how to use the above sources and methods are contained in Part II.

To conclude this discussion of choosing topics, we felt it would be useful to try to anticipate some of the general questions that might crop up on a regular basis. We have chosen four such questions:

- What are the pros and cons of enquiries based on some form of personal involvement?
- Should you choose a topic from the mainstream of sociology or a more unusual one?
- What issues are raised by choosing a social problem as a research enquiry?
- What topics or methods are best avoided?

Personal involvement

There are enormous and obvious attractions, as well as advantages, in the study of an issue or area in which one is personally involved. There are, of course, problems as well. We prefer the word 'problems' here to 'disadvantages'. This is because we want to focus on the fact that all enquiries have problems and that it is your ability to deal with these problems that forms the basis of much of the assessment. In other words, if you can demonstrate that you have recognised and dealt with, or at least taken account of, a problem, you will be rewarded for it. We hope that the notes below will help in this but there are times, also, when an early recognition of problems can lead to a realistic decision against pursuing a particular topic.

First, however, a brief comment on what we mean by personal involvement. It may mean that you simply spend time doing a particular activity (hobby, part-time job etc) but it can mean something that goes beyond this to include significant elements of self-definition or personal belief (eg an adopted child, a policeman's son, a young Mus-

lim woman, a Baptist or whatever). Some of the comments below apply only to certain types of personal involvement.

There is a possible overlap between this discussion of personal involvement projects and those on unusual topics (pages 13-15), or social problem topics (pages 15-20). If this seems likely, then you should consult these sections as well.

We will now look at some of the problems and issues that arise from choosing a topic that's based on personal interest.

Advantages of personal involvement

Interest and commitment

As we discuss in the section on unusual topics, where your research is on a topic you are particularly interested in, it could increase your motivation and commitment to the Enquiry. The research seems relevant to you, not just something you have to do.

Insider knowledge and contacts

Your experiences of the issue in question can be the basis of valuable ideas, research goals or hypotheses. One mature student of ours who was a stepmother sought to follow up experiences of her own to see the extent to which they were common to most stepmothers; common to most mothers; or specific to her own situation. This was a difficult task but very interesting to do and to read and, indeed, extremely well done.

In addition to generating initial ideas and research goals, personal experience and contacts can provide a data source for the whole Enquiry. Parents, other family members, co-worshippers etc could all become interviewees or case studies.

Problems of personal involvement

Thinking as usual

The idea here is one discussed by the phenomeno-logist, Alfred Schütz (1971), in his essay on 'The Stranger'. The basic idea is that being a member of a social group can generate a particular way of thinking, a particular set of beliefs about the world which are taken-for-granted or 'of course' as-sumptions about the world. As Schütz says,

> 'it is the function of the cultural pattern to eliminate troublesome enquiries by offer-ing ready-made directions for use, to re-place truth hard to attain by comfortable truisms and to substitute the self explana-tory for the questionable.'

In other words, if you are too involved in the world you wish to study and cannot detach your-self to play 'the stranger' role sufficiently, you may fail to notice or question issues that your Enquiry should pick up.

Personal commitment

To some extent, this is an elaboration of the pre-vious point. Where you are very committed to a particular belief or very involved in a particular self-definition it may be very unsettling to confront the kinds of questions an outsider would ask.

This may be because of emotional circum-stances. For example, raising questions about being an adopted child may be very difficult emo-tionally. At a practical level here, there are special difficulties in carrying out interviews with family members; can you think of any?

Another difficulty may stem from a commit-ment to a religion which you wish to study.

Sociologists studying religion may not share the absolute belief that a believer or church member does. In itself this is not a problem since sociology and theology offer different levels of under-standing. Nevertheless the devout believer who sees her or his beliefs in terms of transcendental truths may be put off by an approach which looks to the social origins of beliefs. We're not saying that believers are ill-advised to study religion; only that they should be prepared to look at their be-liefs in a different way as sociologists.

Sometimes, of course, commitment to a par-ticular position in society or to a particular set of beliefs can lead one to be partial in selecting and interpreting evidence or to the use of emotive expression. This must be guarded against.

A third area of involvement that could be problematic is where your involvement in, or en-thusiasm for elements of the phenomenon in question can be diverting. This can be the case where you have some specialist knowledge or ex-pertise in the area (eg sport, music) which you naturally want to demonstrate but the knowledge or expertise is of a quite unsociological kind. There is a sociology of football but it isn't particu-larly advanced by an account of how Liverpool are an over-rated team.

Conclusion

In this discussion we have said more about the problems of personal involvement research than about its attractions. But don't let this put you off; a problem becomes an advantage if dealt with well. All enquiries involve risks and opportunities and hopefully this section has indicated some of these for you. Remember, though some topics are best avoided, maybe for personal reasons, the best advice is given in the popular song from the days of your teachers' and grandparents' youth that: 'it ain't what you do it's the way that you do it.'

The mainstream and the unusual

'The sociologist will occupy himself with matters that others regard as too sacred or too distasteful for dispassionate investigation. He will find rewarding the company of priests or prostitutes, depending not on his personal preferences but on the questions he happens to be asking at the moment. He will also concern himself with matters that others find much too boring. He will be interested in the human interaction that goes with warfare or with great intellectual discoveries, but also in relations between people employed in a restaurant or between a group of little girls playing with their dolls.' (Berger 1966)

We could add to this list, sociologists are interested in the sexist assumptions of language, academic or otherwise. The point of this lengthy quote is not, however, to allude to the development of feminist analysis and theory since Berger wrote his book but to highlight the enormous range of issues or areas that a sociologist may choose to study. The same applies to your enquiry. Clearly there are topics which the student researcher cannot or should not contemplate: time, cost, lack of access, considerations of ethics or of personal safety may rule them out; see section on this below (pages 20-21). Nonetheless you are still left with a vast number of possible research topics.

In contemplating your choice, you may well confront the question: is it better to choose a mainstream topic or an unusual, even an exotic

one? Again, there is no right or wrong answer to this but the following observations should help you evaluate any particular decision you are making. These observations are divided into those which point in favour of the unusual and those which do the opposite.

Firstly, however, we should remind you that you are not doing a PhD and that your research does not have to be unique or go into uncharted territory. You will not gain marks for choosing a topic which no one else has covered. Equally, you do not penalise yourself by choosing a topic which is frequently researched by others. We can refer here, to the guidance notes for the London A/S level, 'students should not be expecting or expected to find out anything particularly amazing because the Enquiry is as much about process as well as what is actually produced by the students.' The drift of this comment is probably going to apply to any Enquiry you are likely to be undertaking.

Points in favour of unusual enquiries

Personal challenge and interest

To a large extent this speaks for itself. If your topic is in an unconventional area, or focuses on an unusual aspect of a conventional area, it could give your study a distinctiveness which may be intellectually challenging and personally motivating. It might enable you to look at a personal interest or hobby, which you hadn't previously thought about sociologically, in a completely new way. After all, one of the aims of the AEB syllabus is to give candidates the opportunity 'to apply sociology...to their own experience'. The London A/S has a similar aim.

Scope for the sociological imagination

Whilst the topic choice itself attracts no marks, you may feel a particular choice gives you more scope for demonstrating your ability in areas that are assessed. For example, the AEB syllabus requires a clearly labelled section on the Enquiry Rationale, giving your reasons for choosing the subject, any aims, hypotheses or other observations you wish to make about your topic and its focus. We stress that there is no reason why an unusual topic should score more highly here. But, it's at least possible that doing the unusual may make you think these issues through more fully.

The same applies perhaps to justifying your choice of methods. Being in uncharted seas may encourage you to be more considered and more explicit about your navigation techniques and strategies. (It could, of course, mean that you capsize and drown in a sea of extended metaphors.)

Before moving on to look at the problems of unusual enquiries, we would like to mention a few of the topics chosen and researched with success by our former A level students. By success, we don't mean that they were as good as they could have been but that any limitations were not a direct result of that topic choice or, if they were, the gains outweighed the limitations.

Enquiry 1 - The sociology of the car

This enquiry largely focused on the myth and symbolism of the car both in terms of how it is advertised and, more generally, on how it is bound up with popular conceptions of 'the car and freedom'. This was contrasted with the way the spread of car ownership has undermined the viability of public transport in many areas, thereby reducing freedom for some.

Enquiry 2 - Sociology of Tolkien's 'Middle Earth'

An exploration of a fictional, fantasy society, especially in terms of the themes of social control, power and inequality. Perhaps not a good choice in terms of meeting the assessment objectives of some syllabuses but it does point to how fiction, in literature or elsewhere, can be the subject of sociological study

Enquiry 3 - Women and body building

Research here combined secondary sources (eg literature on the social construction of femininity) with data from relevant sports organisations on the growth of body building among women. Specialist journals were analysed in terms of gender imagery and stereotyping. Case study interviews with a couple of participants were included.

Problems of doing unusual enquiries

Scarcity of material in a sociological form

Whilst you are not likely to rely completely on secondary sources, especially academic literature, as Chapter 3 points out, if there is already some existing literature it could provide ideas for context, approach and methods.

The other side of this coin of absence is, of course, the challenge of devising your own approach and applying sociological concepts and ideas to a topic not usually analysed sociologically.

It is worth remembering that there is a big difference between having enough ideas or information to get started on an Enquiry and being able to get enough data to see it through.

Confidence and self reliance

If you're researching in an area where there is little recognised or published sociological material, it could well be harder to get a 'feel' for what a good enquiry might involve. This may mean that you are less confident of what you're doing, are less able to work at your own pace and are more reliant on the support of your tutor.

With respect to the latter point, we note that the London A/S level marking scheme on *Choice of Topic of Enquiry and Methods* awards marks partly on the degree of assistance the candidate has required. For example, Level One (1-2 marks out of 10) states, 'Required considerable assistance over choice and planning of suitable Enquiry', whereas Level Four (9-10 marks) states, 'Choice of Enquiry required little or no guidance after initial discussions as to its acceptance and development potential.'

We would be very surprised if this meant that the very ambitious student who chose a challenging topic and referred quite frequently to their tutor with informed comments and questions was ruled out of the Level Four mark band. To do so would be to encourage candidates to stay with safe areas.

The AEB coursework memorandum appears more open, referring to:

'guidance in selecting their (ie the candidates') research assignment ... continuing advice and supervision in preparing and pursuing it ... (being) introduced to a variety of research methods and the most appropriate ... Advice ... on how to collect data ... and on the clear presentation, logical structuring, analysis and evaluation of the evidence ... guidance ... on any problems encountered, and to ensure work is kept within reasonable bounds of relevance to the subject.'

In conclusion, always check the Enquiry assessment criteria of the Board whose syllabus you are following. The ability to formulate valid sociological questions will always be in your favour rather than against.

Overall, we would advise you to address these general issues fully in relation to your particular topic choice before you opt for or against an unusual topic. In all Enquiries, whatever the topic area chosen, you should consider carefully the topic's potential and its likely problems, as well as how you might deal with them, before making our final choice.

Social problem enquiries

When we were operating Loughton's Mode 3 A level, it was quite common for students to choose social problems as their topics for research. Sometimes the problem was in the crime/deviancy area, like soccer hooliganism, and sometimes it was in the welfare area, such as an issue to do with old age or disability. Many of these projects were excellent though some fell short of this level because the student had not come to terms with the pitfalls and difficulties that social problem enquiries can present.

The following discussion of the social problem enquiry will tackle both practical and theoretical issues and will be illustrated by reference to other research studies. Its central argument is that the advantages and opportunities of the social problem enquiry generally outweigh the disadvantages, so long as the student is aware of these and approaches the study accordingly.

To begin with, it would be useful to look further at what is meant by a social problem.

Social versus sociological problems

A social problem is not the same thing as a socio-logical problem. According to one writer (Berger 1966), a social problem can be seen to have several elements not found in a sociological problem:

- the application of value judgements; society not working as it ought to be. Many sociologists do not go along with Berger on the question of whether or not sociology can be value free but we won't pursue that here;
- a reliance on the perspectives of the powerful, for it is they who define what counts as a social problem;
- a call for policy or action to change things, to solve the problem.

By contrast, a sociological problem is simply defined as a question of understanding, not judge-ment and action. It concerns how the system overall operates, not why some aspect of it isn't working according to respectable and official opi-nion.

It does not follow from this rather pure dis-tinction that sociologists should adopt a hands-off approach to social problems. Indeed, it would be a pretty poor show for sociology if it couldn't contribute to our understanding of social prob-lems and, indeed, Berger notes that any social action or manipulation - whether seen as benevo-lent or malevolent - could benefit from sociological knowledge or understanding: propa-ganda, fraud, warfare, nursing, slum clearance etc. No, what does follow from Berger's classification is that any sociologist studying social problems has to remember that if she or he only selects from issues already defined as social problems and studies them as they are officially perceived, then they will exhibit a systematic bias in favour of the powerful.

This is bad sociology, not because sociology should side with the underdog, though some argue it should, but rather because it only gives a partial understanding of the phenomenon in question. You may, of course, choose to study official views or policies in relation to a given topic such as acid house parties. That is perfectly OK because your focus is defined in these terms and does not claim to be a study of acid house parties as such.

Some examples of approaches to social prob-lems that illustrate the importance and value of going beyond the official definition of the situation might be useful here:

Poverty and riches

Field (1981) argues that studies of poverty that only focus on the poor miss the point that poverty has to be understood in terms of the overall dis-tribution of income and wealth. He cites the comment of R. H. Tawney, a Fabian Socialist of the early twentieth century, that: 'what thoughtful rich people call the problem of poverty, thoughtful poor people call with equal justice, the problem of riches.' Clearly a political point is being made here, but is it just a political point or a sociological one as well?

Drugs

Young (1971) begins his study of drug use by pointing to the 'artificial barrier' that has been created between legal and illegal drugs. He states that the taken-for-granted assumptions that are involved in this classification lead to ill-informed policies toward both legal (alcohol, tobacco, pres-cribed tranquillizers etc) and illegal drugs. Part of the task of his study is to explore, 'why certain drugs are labelled legal and others totally pro-hibited.' Readers should pick up the interactionist perspective that underlies Young's theoretical stance here.

We are not saying that you always have to broaden out your study so that, for example, all studies of poverty have to include a study of the rich or all studies of a particular illegal drug have to be in the context of a study of all legal drugs as well. What we are saying is that any problem will only be partially understood, and may be grossly misunderstood, if the official or conventional assumptions about it remain completely unchallenged.

Disability and handicap

An interesting follow-up to the last point and a good example of a direct challenge to official and often everyday responses to social problems is provided by a recent advertising campaign. One advert which appeared in a number of daily papers contained several pictures of Parliament. Each image was imperfect in some way, blurred or tunnel shaped, for example. The caption read: 'How the blind see Westminster'. Next to this was a black rectangle with the caption: 'How Westminster sees the blind'. A different and earlier campaign concerned people with disabilities. A bill board poster showed a queue waiting for a job interview. In the queue, we see a wheelchair with a silhouette of a person sitting in it. The caption makes the observation that employers, and others, do not see the person, just the wheelchair.

There are many ways that this campaign data could be used as part of a sociological enquiry. It could, for example, be used in conjunction with research on the number of registered disabled people employed in a particular workplace compared to their numbers nationally; figures for the latter could be obtained from one of the voluntary organisations concerned with disability (see page 30 for advice on how to identify and contact such organisations). Another usage could be as part of an exploration of Goffmans's concept of stigma (Goffman 1968a) in relation to the educational or campaigning strategy of an organisation dealing with disability.

Examples like these remind us that it is the responses of others that often convert disabilities into handicaps and that sociological studies need to reflect this. The point here is that the methods and approaches used by the sociological researcher into the problem of disability should not themselves add to the problem by insensitivity, inappropriateness etc.

Domestic violence

A final example of the limitations of relying on official definitions of social problems comes from Pahl (1985). She notes that, 'there is substantial evidence to suggest that wife-beating has always existed in Britain ...'. However, the condition has only been perceived as a social problem at two periods in British history: '... the late nineteenth century and the post 1971 period.' This points to a useful distinction between the objective elements of a social problem (the actual violence) and the subjective elements (the definition of this by the authorities as unacceptable). Where the former is present but the latter is absent, we can talk of a latent rather than a manifest social problem.

In the case of domestic violence, it was submerged or ignored, says Pahl using Mills' terms, because it was defined as 'a personal trouble of milieu' rather than 'a public issue of social structure'. Just as Mills argues that it was part of the task of sociology to explore the links between individual biography and social and historical circumstances, feminists have sought to show that domestic violence is not just a problem of 'bad husbands' but is related to institutions like the law and ideologies like patriarchy. To take one specific and recent example, some (male dominated?) councils have been reluctant to support battered wives' refuges, characterising them as likely to undermine the family.

Before concluding this section on sociology and social problems, some comments on a more general idea of a social problem approach to sociology is called for. In the 1950s, for example, much sociology of education was focused on the perceived problem of working class underachievement. The basis for this definition came from a mixture of ideas: implicitly functionalist ideas of a wastage of talent being bad for the economy; a liberal philosophy of equality of opportunity; socialist or quasi-socialist ideas of social justice.

It wasn't until feminism began to have an influence on sociology in the 1970s that girls' underachievement in schools relative to boys' was seen as a social problem, gradually gaining some official recognition such as in those sections of the 1975 Sex Discrimination Act dealing with sex discrimination in the curriculum. Hand in hand with this social problem definition of girls' schooling came a growth of sociological research into the topic; gender issues in education had become a sociological problem, though still given more attention by women and feminists than men. We should emphasise here that the sociology of girls and women is not the same as the sociology of gender, though they often are equated.

Similarly, gender role socialisation began to be studied more (sociological problem) as feminists increasingly saw traditional, stereotypical patterns of socialisation as repressive, constraining girls' later opportunities (social problem). What is also clear from this account is that there is not always consensus on what counts as a social problem. Indeed, it is possible to be interested in differential gender role socialisation and approve of such processes.

There are other areas of sociology where the research agenda has reflected social problem perspectives in this wider sense. The historical tendency for youth studies to be of white working class males can partly be seen in terms of the greater social threat they are thought to pose.

The central point that we are making here is that it is not unusual for values to influence the choice of sociological research topics or approaches. It may well be that some notion of justice or some concern for society will influence your topic; this is to be expected. The more you are aware of how your values might affect your approach to this research, the better equipped you will be to avoid the limitations of your taken-for-granted assumptions.

We will now turn from this rather theoretical discussion to some more specific and concrete issues to take note of in choosing and doing a social problem enquiry.

Advantages of social problem enquiry

Available material

The fact that an issue is defined as a manifest social problem and not a latent, unrecognised one means that there will be a range of existing material for the researcher. This can be of various kinds and the researcher should use them in conjunction with the sections later in this book discussing how to interpret and use such data:

- official statistics, documents and reports, including Parliamentary or council chamber debates;
- pressure groups or charities are likely to produce information or possibly be available to you for some primary research (eg interviews). It may be that these organisations have helped bring the issue to public attention and get it defined as a problem; see the role of Shelter on homelessness in the 1960s, for example. Such organisations may be locally or nationally based and this could affect the way you use them;
- media coverage of the above sources and of the problem itself is likely. This may be in specialist journals like *Social Work Today*, the popular press or TV documentaries like *World in Action*. With media reports, bear in mind that sometimes it is the information contained in the report or article that is of interest to you and, at other times, it is the nature of the media coverage that is your focus;
- academic literature on most recognised social problems is fairly readily available.

Personal interest and relevance

Where a topic is one you believe to be of importance because of your personal interest or its relevance to you, you may be more committed to the enquiry. You may be able to gain deeper understanding of the topic in question and, at the same time, give your enquiry a sense of 'ownership'. Remember you don't have to have experienced a problem directly for you to feel it is relevant to you.

Disadvantages of social problem enquiry

The nature of the material available

Though sociologists may well have written accounts of the social problem that is of interest to you, much of the material will have been written neither by nor for sociologists.

Some of the literature, either for the academic or the practitioner in the field, will be from a psychological or even medical perspective, since that is the dominant way that many social problems are approached. This fact alone can be sociologically significant (see pages 46-47) but, after noting this, it leaves you with the choice of ignoring such literature or trying to apply and adapt it sociologically.

Other books will be of a legalistic nature. The law governing your chosen problem can be relevant but you are not likely to need more than the basic framework. Choosing a topic on race and housing, for example, you would need to be aware of the Race Relations Act governing discrimination in this field and possibly some of the limitations of this legislation, but a detailed knowledge or description of the law would not be required. At other times, laws could be cited as examples of the operation or influence of prevailing ideologies, such as the long history of discrimination against women in social security legislation. Once again, the technicalities of the law would not be required.

Some other literature may be oriented to bureaucratic or administrative procedures, such as those for taking a child into care. A description of such procedures may be given in condensed form but it would only become more relevant if you could draw out points of sociological significance in your account of these procedures - eg:

What role do parents have in care proceedings? Where, if at all, might the process be influenced by assumptions about the child's background (family, class, ethnicity) or gender? The section on the use of non-sociological literature (pages 45-50) will be useful here.

Value judgements

As we have noted above, the mere definition of a topic as a social problem involves a value judgement, even though the value judgement may not be one you share. For example, one parent families are sometimes defined as problems. This definition is rejected by an opposing viewpoint which asserts that, whilst one parent families may *experience* problems they should not be defined as *being* problems. Indeed they might argue that one of the problems one parent families experience is the definition of them as problems - singling them out for prejudice or comment for example (see *Social Studies Review* 1990).

Whether the value judgements are yours or somebody else's, the more you are aware of them the better. If they are your own, try to keep them to a minimum; you won't get marks for saying poverty is an awful thing. If you do make value judgements, try to link them to your data. For example, if you say that the government should rely less on means-tested benefits, don't say it is because you think they are not high enough. Rather you should link it to some research or at least an hypothesis about how they actually operate, such as stigma and low take-up rate, for example. If you wish to stress the harshness of such a policy you could make factual comparisons with current levels of wages or levels of benefit in the past to make your point and use words like 'lower' rather than emotive words like 'harsh' or 'mean'. Alternatively you may cite the views of a pressure group or charity which argues the 'meanness' case, but here you are legitimately reporting the value positions of social actors/groups, not making your own value judgements. But you must show you know when you are doing this.

You should not feel obliged to suggest solutions to the problems you are studying. However, if you can suggest some policies which are based on sociological knowledge and understanding rather than political judgements or personal feelings, this is generally acceptable.

There is one area in the study of social problems where you should exercise value judgements. This is in the carrying out of any primary research you may do. Whether doing interviews or observation, remember that the people that you are researching are not objects or animals in a zoo; they have rights and feelings, including the right to refuse to be researched. Perhaps here it is useful to recall our earlier observation that the source of many people's social problems lies not within themselves, nor in the stars, but within the structures and attitudes of wider society. This refers to the point made earlier (page 17) about sociologists being part of the social world and, if they aren't careful, their actions as researchers can become part of the process by which people, such as those with disabilities, are insensitively treated or labelled by wider society. In doing so they are converting a disability into a handicap (see McNeill 1990).

Enquiries best avoided

To some degree, the discussion of various types of enquiry - personal involvement etc - has already raised the question of what topics are best avoided. Whether a topic is inadvisable or completely out of the question depends on the topic, the method and the person carrying it out. There are a range of general factors that you should take account of in making your decision.

Clearly, there are practical ones, like the availability of data or the difficulties of gathering it yourself. These are discussed in relation to particular research methods. Questions of scale (size, time span) and cost rule out some topics or approaches as do the practical difficulties of access (eg studies of the very wealthy - unless you are rich!).

As important, however, are personal ones and we are not just referring to emotional questions as discussed above. Some projects or methods are best avoided for reasons of personal safety or legality. Seeking to interview members of extreme right wing or racist organisations or to observe football hooliganism too closely are obvious examples of the former. Asking people whether they take illegal drugs could be an example of both. Remember too that your age can be a factor in which activities are legal or not.

Related to this is the important question of ethics. In gathering data, the ends do not always justify the means. In *Endless Pressure* (1979), Ken Pryce was ambivalent about his decision to 'con-vert' in order to study a religious group and thus to exploit their trust.

Such covert research may be relatively harmless compared to the possible ways that observation or inappropriate interviewing may be employed in the study of particular social groups - whether they be inmates of residential institutions or in some other respect a member of a vulnerable or even stigmatised group.

One of the contributions of feminism to sociology has been to push the question of the relationship between the researcher, the researched and the topic itself further up the sociological agenda. With this in mind, you might usefully ask of your enquiry and proposed research method: what effect will this have on the people I am studying?

Conclusion

Social problems can be interesting topics for sociological enquiries with great scope for a wide use of secondary sources as well as primary research.

However, great care over the approach to these sources needs to be exercised. In particular, avoid the wholesale inclusion of non-sociological material and remember that 'doing good' or 'being nice' are not usually contained in the assessment objectives of examination boards.

CHECKLIST - CHOOSING YOUR ENQUIRY

 Have you **focused narrowly enough** or are you attempting to cover too broad an area?

Will you be able to gather **enough information** from your own research or from other sources to justify the original choice?

 Are you able to study the topic in a sufficiently sociological way or will you end up writing an enquiry which is **accurate and informative but not sociological?**

Is the topic going to **keep you interested** and involved?

Have you considered all the **personal, emotional, legal and ethical issues involved** in the research, both for yourself and for others?

2

Planning and doing the enquiry

Good organisation is the key to success in enquiry work. You may spend as long as a year working on it and collect, en route, a large quantity of information. Because it's a more substantial undertaking than, say, an essay, good organisation is more important in this than in other types of sociological writing that you do on your course. Without it, it's all too easy to lose direction, flounder under a mass of data and lose heart in the whole process.

Self-motivation is a key requirement of project work. We each develop our own ways of sustaining interest in a project. Ultimately there are no right or wrong ways of studying, but some methods are better than others. One strategy most of us have been guilty of one time or another is to leave things to the last minute - working at a frenzied rate just before the deadline.

The 'blind panic' approach may have worked for you in the past but our experience with students doing A level sociology projects is that even the very able make a mess of a rushed project. But to keep up interest and motivation over a longer time period you need a clear sense of direction and to be well-planned so that you can confirm that you are making progress. Of course, it's also important to choose a topic that will sustain your interest throughout the research period (see Chapter 1 for more advice on this).

In any project there will be periods when you feel demoralised and that you will never be finished, periods of exhilarating progress, and a lot of routine 'plodding'. Professional sociologists will admit to similar experiences. It is important that you set yourself a regular routine for working on the enquiry, perhaps a particular time each week and that you stick to it. Reviving interest in something you have put aside for weeks or even months is very hard!

Set a sensible target for each study period before you begin so that you have a clear idea of what you should have achieved by the end of the study session. The more active and purposeful you are, the more likely it is that you will make progress. For example, you might decide that in a two hour session you will write a draft interview schedule, or you will use class notes and relevant texts to produce a summary of the strengths and weaknesses of a particular research technique.

The need for clear aims applies particularly to the use of books and other documents (see also section on reading, recording and writing, pages 33-35). Read actively, that is have a clear idea of the questions and issues that you are interested in. It's helpful to write these down before you start to avoid getting sidetracked. This will allow you to work through the material effectively and quickly, skipping irrelevant sections and getting at the bits which are necessary for your purposes. You may, of course, be gripped by inspiration and exceed your original target but if you are unclear about what you expect to achieve it's all too easy to end up staring at the wallpaper glassy-eyed and frustrated.

It's advisable to avoid long study sessions. According to psychological research, maximum attention span is normally between thirty and forty-five minutes. After that concentration begins to fade. Therefore, breaks of five or ten minutes, at regular intervals, will improve your productivity. You will gain most benefit from these breaks if you have a complete change of activity - make a cup of coffee, go for a short walk etc.

Involving other people in the enquiry is another way of keeping your interest alive and fresh. Take every opportunity you can of discussing the issues you're working on with other people - fellow students and non-sociologists may come up with insights which are helpful or suggest new lines of enquiry.

Group work on enquiries

A word on group work is relevant here. The AEB syllabus allows group projects '...up to and including the data collection stage of a study. The write up by the candidate of all stages should, however, be the individual work of the candidate' (AEB guidance notes for coursework).

Working with others in this way has a number of benefits. You have the stimulus of others' ideas, you can divide some of the tasks between you (preparatory reading, contacting organisations and other research sources, monitoring the press or television programmes etc) and you could conduct a larger primary research programme than would be possible on your own. But you will first need to give careful thought to whether you work better with others or alone, who else is on the team, whether they will pull their weight, whether you will function effectively as a team - heated disagreements can be productive but they can also be highly disruptive!

AEB guidelines also state: 'There is no prohibition on students from the same centre choosing to study the same topic.' One strategy

---

ACTIVITY 2 - GROUP THINKTANK ON ENQUIRIES

One activity that's very useful whatever your topic is a 'thinktank' - a group session on enquiries. This is a class devoted to individual progress reports on the enquiry where everyone can make critical comments, give advice and make suggestions.
You'll find that this can be very useful, and not only when your own work is being discussed, but also listening and contributing to the discussion of others'.

Group 'thinktanks' can be valuable at various stages in the enquiry: at the 'choosing' stage, a session on provisional enquiry proposals can generate ideas on approaches, methods and sources; when your research procedure is more developed, on design flaws, fine tuning of methods etc; when your research is completed, on how to handle your findings, relevant theoretical issues and debates, evaluation and so on.

that you might consider together as a group when you are selecting enquiry topics could be to establish group cooperation between students working in related topic areas to reflect on common issues and themes. For example, a group of students working on individual enquiries in the field of education, gender or 'social problems' (see pages 15-20) could explore background issues and exchange core ideas while pursuing their own particular lines of inquiry. In the same way regular feedback sessions, where individuals can report on, and the group can discuss, the progress of individual pieces of student research can be very useful. Professional researchers nearly always collaborate in this manner.

Your tutor is probably the best person to help organise such group activities although there is nothing to stop you going ahead on your own. However, do check carefully the requirements of the examining board. The London Board does **not** allow group projects so collective work on the same piece of research is prohibited under their scheme. This would not necessarily rule out the sort of thematic collaboration between students working in related areas which is described above. You should take advice from your teacher (who may need to consult the Board) before embarking on any collective activity to avoid breaching the regulations of the relevant examining board.

Time management

An important feature of good organisation is to plan ahead. Some research activities will take much longer than you expect. For instance, devising an interview schedule, piloting it on a small sample of individuals, selecting your research sample, contacting respondents, arranging interview dates, conducting interviews, re-contacting

unavailable respondents, and coding and analysing your results is a process which will take many weeks from beginning to end - see Chapter 8 for further advice on this.

Similarly, contacting and extracting relevant information from a pressure group may take several letters and follow-up phone calls, or interviews. There will often be delays while you wait for replies, so all activities of this sort should be initiated as soon as possible after you have decided upon a research topic and strategy.

It's often possible to have several research activities running in parallel. Suppose you were doing an enquiry on *The Media Reaction to Acid House Parties*. You might begin preparatory reading, contacting relevant organisations, and monitoring press and broadcasting coverage of the issue all within the first few weeks of your research.

You will see from this that organising your research activities can become complicated. This is especially true where you need to have completed one activity before you can begin the next. Professional project managers often use project planning calendars to organise and display the most efficient sequence of activities and you may find it helpful to use one of these. You can buy these from commercial stationery suppliers or make one up for yourself.

Wherever your research depends on access to a particular organisation or group (eg a local school or members of a youth subculture) it is vital to make contact as early as possible in the research process. Don't leave your first approach to the last minute, only to find, as one of our students did, that no one at the primary school had time to be interviewed because they were going all-out for the production of the Christmas panto! Beware of

SOCIOLOGY ENQUIRY PROPOSAL FORM

PROVISIONAL TITLE:

'Acid House Parties: The Growth of a New Subculture'.

AIMS/OBJECTIVES/HYPOTHESES:

1. Brief historical account of growth of Acid House Parties and the social reaction to them.

2. What sociological explanations can be found for this movement?

3. Describe and explain the social reaction to Acid House Parties (perhaps looking at press, broadcasting, police treatment etc).

PROPOSED METHODS:

1. Content analysis of coverage in selected media over one month including music press.

2. Interviews with participant and/or possibly direct observation.

3. Style analysis of some acid house lyrics or LP, CD or cassette covers.

SOURCES, CONCEPTS AND REFERENCES

1. Moral panic analysis: Cohen, S (1973) *Folk Devils and Moral Panics.*

2. Subcultural theory: Willis, P. (1970) *Profane Culture.*

3. Lyric analysis: Harker, D. (1980) *One for the Money.*

4. Music magazines and press reports as 'witting' and 'unwitting' evidence (see pages 41-43).

INITIAL PLAN OF ACTION

Getting started

Topic decided in summer term:

1. During summer term, begin sociological background reading on subcultures and youth movements, identify key sociological concepts and theories (see above).

2. Start literature search for articles and references to acid house phenomenon using *British Humanities Index* etc (see section on using the library for more details on indexes).

Researching and analysing

Over the summer break:

3. Begin scanning current media output for relevant material (TV, films, promo videos etc).

4. Collect material from your selected sources for content analysis.

5. Plan and pilot interview schedules, or design observational strategy.

During autumn term:

6. Formal submission of project proposals.

7. Construct content analysis categories and begin analysing media reports using these.

8. Conduct interviews/observation.

During Christmas break:

9. Draft enquiry for discussion with your tutor.

Organisation and presentation

During spring term:

10. Discuss draft with tutor.

11. Write up final version of your enquiry.

The above is an example but don't follow it rigidly as the demands of your enquiry may well be different. We have assumed here that the student researcher is following a two year course. You will need to compress your plans if you are a one year A level student. Remember, at each stage, your tutor will be there to advise you and comment on your proposals.

making the assumption that respondents have nothing else to occupy their time and of overestimating their willingness to drop everything to assist your enquiry. Allow sufficient time to secure their cooperation, offering alternative times and venues. Respondents will be more cooperative if you explain carefully the purpose of your research, and a letter from a tutor may also help in the first instance.

Finally, don't forget to send 'thank you' letters to those who have helped you. It may be a good idea to offer a summary of your findings, but be prepared to accept criticism if you do. If your informants are involved in the research process they are more likely to be helpful.

Enquiry proposal and plan of action

It is essential that you devise a plan of action. This is a list of things to be done in the order they need to be tackled. The plan of action should include estimates of the time required for each activity (see relevant chapters in Part II for more information on this) and indicate the sequence in which these should be carried out.

It's difficult to lay down hard and fast rules for this as much will depend on the type of enquiry and the nature of the research activities involved. Certainly you should begin with a search of the literature, background reading and the identification of relevant concepts, theories and research strategies. At the end of the research period allow extra time for 'slippage' (things going wrong, uncooperative respondents, changes in direction of research etc) and for writing up the enquiry, which will almost certainly take longer than you anticipate.

Even though your plan of action will depend on the nature of your own enquiry, certain dates

will be predetermined. The deadline for the submission of your completed enquiry will be set by the relevant examining body. In the case of the AEB, enquiries have to be assessed by your teacher(s) and the marks sent to the board by 1st April of the year in which the examination is to be taken. Effectively this means work will be required for marking at least two or three weeks before this date, possibly more if it is a large centre and marks have to be agreed between several members of staff as required by the board. The London Board requires work to be sent to them by 1st May and so a similar interval for marking will need to be set before this date.

Examining boards may also set a date by which project proposals/outlines (more on these later) must be submitted. The London Board requires these to be submitted for approval by 1st November (2 year courses) or 31st December (1 year courses) in the calendar year before the exam is to be taken. Proposals do not have to be sent for approval by the AEB. The requirements of other boards were not known at the time of writing.

Even if there is no board requirement to submit a project proposal before going ahead with a project, it is good practice to produce one, indeed your school or college may have designed its own. If not, the sample form on page 26 may be helpful. Discuss your proposal with your tutor before you go ahead with your project - it's important to check that she or he thinks that your planned enquiry is feasible before you start on the serious work of data collection.

The enquiry log

Keeping a log of the progress of your project is another useful way to organise yourself through the research process. If you are following the syllabus of the London Board a log is required and forms part of the work on which you will be assessed.

The log should record the development of your ideas and the accumulation of information, changes in direction, focus or methodology that occur. It should also reflect on problems and obstacles that arose during the research period and comment on how you dealt with them. Remember, it is a sociological record of issues, experiences and events as they happen. Therefore, you should also make some attempt to explain what happened in sociological terms. Don't just record that you wrote to, say, *Friends of the Earth* but that they didn't reply. For example, you would get more credit for weighing up why some pressure groups are more able than others to respond to such requests for information.

In this way, the log forms a valuable record of work-in-progress and the development of your thought which will be very useful when you come to write the final report. It helps you to document developments that you need to comment upon later but which can easily be forgotten if not recorded.

Thus we recommend that you keep a log, making regular entries right from the start of the enquiry even if, as in the case of the AEB syllabus, it is not assessed along with your research report. Another function of the log is that it provides a starting point and focus for tutorial discussions - it's one way that you can make the most effective use of your tutor's advice and it will help you to identify the areas in which you require further help and guidance (see also section on *Getting advice* pages 35-36).

Using the library

Whatever your enquiry topic, the library is an important resource. To make the best use of the library as an information source you need to understand how it works so that you can search for and retrieve materials efficiently. You will need, of course, to know how the library classification system works.

Most libraries use the Dewey system of classification by subject. You will probably know that, under this system, most sociology books are to be found between 300-309. But do not restrict your search to these areas alone. There are major areas of sociology which are normally shelved at other locations (educational sociology at 370, crime at 360 and so on).

The Dewey subject index will tell you ALL the locations where books on a particular topic are to be found. A topic such as 'drugs' has a number of different entries under it: chemical analysis, medical applications, medical misuse, drug addiction, legal aspects, sociology, health aspects. Not all of these will be relevant to a sociological enquiry on the topic, but it would be a mistake to assume that the only useful information is to be found under the sociology section.

Also, always ask the librarian but give them notice of anything more than the simplest enquiry. They want (and are paid) to help in information searching.

The reference section

Here you will find a number of works of direct sociological importance such as *Social Trends, Regional Trends, The Annual Abstract of Statistics.* There is more on the application of these publications to student enquiries later (see Chapter 5). But there are a number of non-sociological refer-

USEFUL REFERENCE WORKS	
ORGANISATIONS	
Directory of Pressure Groups Directory of British Associations Charities Digest Directory of Voluntary Organisations Social Services Yearbook Yellow pages and Thomson classified telephone directories	Contain lists of organisations which may be useful in your research. Some have useful regional and subject indexes - Directory of British Associations classifies organisations by subject so you can look up organisations concerned with vegetarianism or the blind. They have names and addresses, telephone numbers so that you can make contact.
PRESS AND OTHER JOURNALS	
Willings Press Guide Brad Directories & Annuals Benn Press Guide	List titles, publishers, circulations, group ownership etc. The Brad guide also lists media provision by area for the UK and Europe.
INDEXES TO ARTICLES	
British Humanities Index Clover Applied Social Science Index and Abstracts	List articles published in newspapers and journals by subject. Eg can look up all articles on particular topic. Many journals, and some newspapers, have their own subject index.
TELEVISION	
Newsbrief	Monthly BBC index to a video compilation of BBC television news, has information on the timing of stories - could be useful for a simple content analysis (see pages 58-63).
LIBRARY SERVICES	
Press Cuttings Files	Many libraries offer a press cutting service. You may be able to request a cuttings file to be opened on your research topic. Cuttings will normally be retrospective - usually there is a delay before cuttings are taken which underlines the need to begin your research promptly. Small libraries usually can't afford to take every paper so range may be limited.
Library staff	Library staff are highly skilled in the retrieval of information - their advice can be invaluable.

ence books which can be very useful in your research (see the box on page 30).

Beyond the library walls

So far we have assumed that you have access to your school, college or local libraries but the resources of other libraries and information banks can also be arranged. If your library is equipped with a computer you may be able to use this to search for information in large computer files. British Telecom's *Prestel* or *Campus 2000* database is accessible in many libraries and can be searched by simple 'keywords'. You will probably need the advice of the librarian to make use of these facilities.

Most libraries also have facilities for inter-library loans and through this mechanism you can have access to a massive range of materials - even unpublished doctoral theses! The process of arranging inter-library loan material can be lengthy, so again an early start is essential if you are to make effective use of this service.

Helpful organisations

Don't overlook other organisations which can point you in the right direction. For example, the Town Hall, the local radio station, the community relations council, the legal aid centre and organisations such as the *Commission for Racial Equality,* and the *Equal Opportunities Commission* may have lists of small or 'alternative' organisations. They may also be able to put you in touch with local branches of national organisations.

SKIMMING, SCANNING, RECEPTIVE & REFLECTIVE READING		
	DEFINITION	*USES*
Skimming	very rapid, not reading every word, running your eyes over text, picking up keywords, headings, illustrations etc.	useful way to gather a quick impression of a chapter, get the main sense of what it's about, whether more careful reading necessary
Scanning	similarly fast but more focused - looking for particular ideas, words or phrases	suitable for locating relevant sections for further study
Receptive	reading at normal comprehension speed, faster than speech	suitable for text which is fairly easily comprehended
Reflective reading	close and careful study of the text, much slower than receptive reading	necessary where text is complex or unfamiliar

SQ3R: SURVEY, QUESTION, READ, RECALL AND REVIEW

SURVEY	A quick initial skim of the section to gain an overall impression of its contents, length and so on. Make use of the title, contents page, prefaces, forewords or introductions, summaries and conclusions, the index, bibliography and references
QUESTION	Note down some questions that you want answered by the text. Your reading will be much more focused and efficient if you are clear about what you're looking for. What questions arise from your enquiry plan? What do you know already on the subject? What is the author's theoretical perspective? Make your own list before you start.
READ	Without taking notes read through the section you are interested in at a comfortable speed for understanding applying the questions you devised above and others which may arise.
RECALL	Stop at regular intervals for recall - especially if the text is difficult. Close the book and try to remember the main points making notes in your own words to help you. The latter helps you to understand and reduces the risk of plagiarism - copying the work of another author. Enquiries that are plagiarised will, of course, get no marks.
REVIEW	Check the accuracy of your recall (it's a good idea to assume that you've missed something), check and update your notes against the text making sure you have answered the questions you began with.

Sample index cards

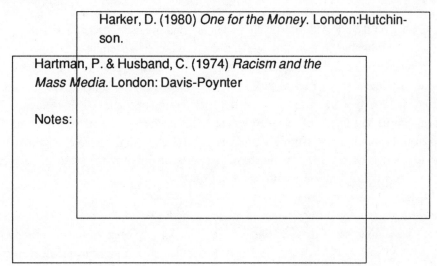

Harker, D. (1980) *One for the Money*. London:Hutchinson.

Hartman, P. & Husband, C. (1974) *Racism and the Mass Media*. London: Davis-Poynter

Notes:

Specialist libraries

It's usually very easy to gain permission to use the library of your local polytechnic or university for reference purposes. This means you have access to library facilities (books, journals etc) but are not allowed to borrow material. You may be asked to provide a letter from your tutor as evidence that you are a bona fide student. This will give you access to a very wide range of specialist, academic publications.

It is possible to arrange similar facilities at specialist libraries such as the Millicent Fawcett library (women) in London, the Wilberforce Library (slavery) at Hull University or various government libraries (eg the Department of Education and Science). The *Guide to Government Libraries* and the *Public Libraries and Museums Yearbook* (in the reference section of your library) will help you locate these and the librarian may help you to arrange permission to use their materials.

A word of caution. If you do use a specialist library you must be very clear about what information you are after - it's easy to sink in such deep oceans of knowledge. Unless you're interested in a particularly specialist or obscure area the resources of your local library will probably be sufficient.

Reading, recording and writing

This section contains some hints on how to develop these three skills which are central to project and enquiry work.

Reading

Quite often people feel overwhelmed by the amount of reading they have to come to grips with as student researchers. We learn the basics at primary school but it's rare for schools to provide any further training. But, reading is not just one activity but many. You have only to consider the different ways you read a poem, a textbook, the *Radio Times,* or a novel. Have a look at the box on page 31 which describes the differences between 'skimming', 'scanning', 'receptive' and 'reflective' reading. Clearly, in the interests of efficiency, you should spend the minimum time in slow, reflective reading. Thus you will only have to struggle with reading that is relevant to your enquiry.

It's possible to find out a lot about a book without reading it! The title is, of course, one clue, but read also the publisher's 'blurb': a brief description of content on the cover of most books. Contents pages will help you to identify relevant sections. Check whether any issues, names or concepts that you are interested in are indexed at the back - look these up to see if they are likely to be helpful.

Finally, prefaces and bibliographies can sometimes give a clue to the writer's point of view and are worth scanning. All this should take no more than 5 minutes.

Taking notes from books involves several separate activities and one can easily get in the way of the others. The SQ3R technique is a well established sequence which may be helpful here. It takes a little practice to get the best from this technique but it's worth persevering.

Recording

Over the period of your enquiry you will probably read quite a lot of material. As a consequence, it's

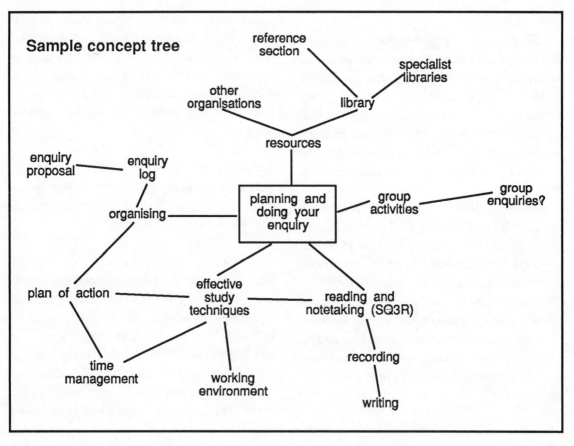

Sample concept tree

important to develop a system for storing your notes. Many researchers find a card index system helpful. Each card should record the author (surname and initial), date of publication, title, and publisher. For articles you should also record the name of the journal, the volume and issue number (see page 33 for an example).

Recording all this information now saves a lot of time when you come to list your references at the end of your project. It's very tedious searching for a book or article, just in order to find out the exact title, or date of publication. The card will also contain your notes taken as you read.

If you follow this system it's often possible to construct the text of your enquiry report by re-arranging the sequence of the cards. Of course, the cards are not essential, a looseleaf file is just as good, but avoid using both sides of the paper or card, and don't use bound notebooks as it's harder to rearrange the information later on.

Writing

Writing is never easy, but the better organised you are the fewer problems you should experience. Again, it's helpful to view writing as three separate activities: invention, drafting and revising.

Invention

The most important of these is invention. This is the time you spend being creative, and brain-storming ideas. The one rule here is that you put down everything that comes to mind - even the most unlikely idea. Change nothing, just allow your mind to wander around the topic. By this method you will generate a lot of worthless ideas and a few gems. But you will never get any gems if you are too self critical - the whole purpose of this stage is to let the ideas flow. Professional writers

will often spend half of their writing time on this part of the process.

When you've finished, sort these ideas into some sort of plan. A concept tree (see page 34) can be useful because it compresses a lot of information, lets you see the whole at a glance and clarifies the relationships between ideas.

Drafting

Drafting should be fairly quick, don't over-correct, just get the ideas down and worry about expression, spelling and punctuation later.

Drafting should take less than 25% of your writing time leaving the final quarter for revision. Here you can alter the sequence of arguments, correct and edit your grammar and spelling.

If you have access to one, a word processor makes these stages much easier. Try typing with the screen turned off so that you can't change or censor your flow of thoughts during the invention stage, for example.

Revising

Revising is the stage where you delete sections and move them into a better sequence (scissors and paste or using the block editing facilities of a word processor).

Once the general shape of the enquiry is in place, revise again, this time for expression, grammar, spelling and so on. From this you can produce the final version. See also Chapter 9 on the presentation, structure and conclusions of the enquiry.

Getting advice

The examiners do not expect you to do the project entirely without guidance. The London Board, for example, assumes that students will need and be entitled to receive advice from tutors through all stages of the project. This includes comment and advice on:

- the selection of the project,
- its main areas of investigation,
- the collection, organisation of material,
- the use and evaluation of material.

(ULSEB Guidance Notes for Sociology AS) Similar notes from the AEB state that:

'Candidates may be given guidance during the course of the study on any problems encountered, and to ensure that work is kept within reasonable bounds of relevance to the subject.'

Therefore it's a good idea to have regular meetings with your tutor to discuss the progress of your work. You might find it useful to indicate these at appropriate points in your plan of action. Your tutor will be able to help you plan your work between tutorial sessions, helping you to define targets and set interim deadlines.

In the last analysis, of course, you will be assessed on the written work that you produce. But the tutor is there to take your initial ideas about where you're going and suggest ways that you might develop them, to give guidance on the best paths, the pitfalls and the blind alleys. You can take all the advice you wish, and it's best that you do, but in the end it's you that has to make the journey and it's your performance here that is marked.

You won't get good grades from slavishly following the suggestions of your tutor, but good advice frequently sought and put to use with initiative and flair will give you the best chance of success.

CHECKLIST - PLANNING AND DOING THE ENQUIRY

 What possibilities are there for you to take advantage of **group collaboration** on some aspect of your enquiry?

 Are you certain that you have made the most **effective use of your library's resources?**

 Does your enquiry proposal indicate the main **approaches, methods, relevant sociological concepts** and **sources of information?**

 Have you made a **plan of action**; kept your **enquiry log** up to date and does it provide an ongoing record of the development of your ideas?

 Have you set up and kept to a **systematic method for recording the information** you collect?

Part II

Researching and analysing

Includes

Introduction to Part II

Using books

Using the media

Statistical sources

Documents

Observation

Questionnaires and interviews

Introduction to Part II

Sociological theories and methods

In the next six chapters we look in some detail at a number of research methods which you may draw upon when carrying out your enquiry. Before we begin, there are a number of general issues concerning sociological theory and research methods which should first be discussed. This will clarify some of the underlying assumptions of the chapters which follow, although we will return to some of these issues in more specific terms when looking at particular methods.

What is primary research?

It's common in sociology texts to find a distinction made between primary data, collected directly by the researcher, and data which comes from secondary sources, that is from the work of other researchers. Under this classification primary data would include information obtained by questionnaires, interviews and observation, secondary data would include the use of sociological findings, information collected for other purposes by government departments, pressure groups, the mass media and so on.

We are unhappy with this distinction because it is based on where the information comes from rather than how it is used. The point is made well by Marwick (1977) who argues that there is a difference between what he calls the *witting* and *unwitting* use of evidence:

'witting evidence is evidence which the original author of the document intended to impart. Unwitting evidence is everything else that can be learned from the document.'

You may, for example, use reports in the media as a direct source of information on a topic. A press interview with an alcoholic or heroin user could be used to illustrate a particular sociological theory of addiction; a television documentary on homelessness may provide useful statistics to support your investigation of that topic.

Government reports or official statistics can be used in the same direct way. For example, the *Beveridge Report* (1942) provides much information on the social conditions of the day and the situation of those in need. Similarly official statistics on, for instance, the numbers entering higher education, rates of divorce, or the take up of state benefits may be used as direct evidence in different enquiries.

These are all examples of what Marwick calls witting evidence; evidence that is used in the same way as the original author intended. But Marwick's distinction alerts us to the fact that reports, documents, statistics and research can also be used in ways that were not intended by the author as unwitting evidence. Thus a television programme can be analysed to produce evidence of stereotyping, suicide statistics can be used to reveal coroners' beliefs concerning the cause of suicide, the report of a pressure group can be probed to reveal an underlying set of assumptions and ideology.

In these examples the same material is transformed from a source of information into a topic in its own right. When we use material in this second way as unwitting evidence, it becomes primary research.

In the chapters which follow we define primary research in terms of how material is used rather than where it comes from. Certainly we encourage the use of multiple methods, primary as well as secondary research, in your inquiry. But, remember that primary research does not have to consist of questionnaires, interviews or observation. There are times when it will be more appropriate to do primary research by looking for unwitting evidence in material produced by others.

Numbers or people?

Methodological theory is sometimes presented in terms of 'goodies' and 'baddies'. On the one hand there are the wicked positivists, naively using methods which quantify, treat people as objects, and which force meaning upon social action rather than seeking to discover and understand it. Posed against this are the beleaguered band of heroic phenomenologists, for whom numbers are an irrelevance, using the humane and sensitive arts of empathy. They, by contrast, want to get inside their subjects and to look out at the world through their eyes.

The mythical confrontation between positivists and phenomenologists has now become part of sociological folklore, told in sociological texts

and retold in many an A level essay. However, it is relevant to a discussion of the research methods used in your enquiry. This is because different research methods are frequently attached to one or other of the opposing theoretical camps.

Thus official statistics are seen as 'tainted' data and any attempt to quantify is condemned as positivistic. Interviews (except perhaps the informal, unstructured kind) and questionnaires are similarly rejected out of hand.

Our concern is that you do not choose research strategies for your enquiry on the basis of this simplistic and stereotyped view. The following comments may clarify the situation:

- Methods are not 'good' or 'bad' in themselves. What is important is how they are used. If you were building a log cabin, you probably wouldn't claim that a saw was a better tool than a hammer; each has its own purpose. Much the same can be said for sociological methods; the 'tools' of sociology. Rather, you should be aware of the strengths and weaknesses of different methodological approaches, where they are appropriate and where they are not.

- Many professional sociologists use not one but many methods of research. Although his main method was participant observation, Pryce's (1979) study of West Indian communities in Bristol is a good example. He mentions a range of other sources: books, parliamentary papers, monographs, back copies of the *Bristol Evening Post*, official documents published by Bristol City Corporation, probation officer files and interviewing.

- Not all sociologists use such a diverse range of methods, although many do. Rather than persisting with the mythical struggle between positivism and phenomenology, Pawson (1989) argues that a more accurate alternative is to classify researchers into 'purists' and 'pragmatists'. The former stick persistently to one methodology (positivism or phenomenology) while the latter, like Pryce, use a blend of strategies using data from official statistics, for example, to qualify or support interview data. Although the scope of your enquiry will be much smaller, we recommend the pragmatic approach to the selection of methods for your enquiry. If you use several methods you have more opportunities to demonstrate your understanding of different forms of research. The pragmatic approach also helps you evaluate your findings by comparing different forms of evidence.

- Most sociologists would agree that there is nothing wrong with quantification when used appropriately. David Silverman (1986) is a longstanding critic of positivism in sociology. He argues that there is nothing inconsistent between the phenomenologist's approach which seeks to understand how actors define and interpret the world, and quantification. Indeed, he argues, ethnographic approaches are often flawed by their lack of hard quantitative data with which to ground their generalisation. At times, he says: 'the critical reader is forced to ponder whether the researcher has selected only those fragments of data which support his argument.' He goes on to say that quantification, used appropriately, is a desirable feature of any research: 'The point, then, is to count the countable, preferably in terms of the categories actually used by the participants.'

3

Using books

'I do not like to do empirical research if I can possibly avoid it.' Mills (1970)

In this quote from *The Sociological Imagination* Mills is pointing to the fact that, on many topics of sociological interest, there already exists a considerable volume of published material. Good sociology, he argues, is as much about ways of understanding data as it is about collecting it. It is certainly not about gathering data for its own sake, with no sense of what the data is being collected for. Where a body of information already exists, the sociologist's task is to select those aspects which are relevant to her or his research, to suggest and look for connections and patterns and to search for explanations.

The same applies to your enquiry. It is quite possible that your chosen topic can be perfectly adequately explored using published sources. Some topics may lend themselves to this rather than personal or primary research. Alternatively, you may have opted for an enquiry based mainly on primary research, but even here reference to published material can be extremely valuable and, in most cases, essential.

Before going on to look at the uses you may make of books and the things to bear in mind when using them, a few cautionary points need to be made, particularly regarding enquiries based mainly on published sources.

It is important to remember that most syllabuses will include some assessment of the ability to demonstrate a knowledge and understanding of research methods relevant to or used in the enquiry. If you haven't carried out any primary research, you need to consider the nature and value of your sources in these terms. This doesn't mean that you have to look at every book or article's research methods in detail but it does mean you cannot simply list a summary of key findings. Be guided by the syllabus assessment objectives on this.

On this general comment it is worth noting the comment of Shipman (1988):

'A most alarming development is the proliferation of "readers" presenting extracts from a number of sources on a subject. Another is the production of simple, filleted versions for students. These present the core of the original without any of the accompanying description of methods and their shortcomings which appear in the original. No opportunity or invitation is given to assess reliability or validity. Students and public fed on a diet of readers and popular accounts would have little idea of the real nature of social science.'

Having said this, we do feel that such books can have a role in your enquiry work. For example, they can give an idea of what sociological concepts and theories have been employed in relation to a given topic - but they should be seen as springboards not mattresses.

We now outline a number of ways in which books, or other publications, can be used in enquiry work and some things to bear in mind when using or evaluating these sources. Mostly, of course, these texts will be works of sociology although we also discuss the use of non-sociological books, especially those of related disciplines like history or psychology, but the points raised could be applied to the use of any literature from school geography text books to works of fiction or drama. Our starting point is that a useful, though not watertight distinction can be made between using books as sources of data and using them as sources of ideas.

Books as sources of data

The data available from published sources can be valuable in several ways. It may, for example, provide much of the main body of your findings. This might particularly be the case where your chosen topic requires some historical or cross-cultural data, or where you have chosen to study a relatively closed social world. For most students, the world of the very rich comes into this category and whilst stories about wealthy individuals may get newspaper coverage, the political role of wealth may not. You might find that writing to the Queen for help in an enquiry, as a former O level student of ours once did, was not substantially rewarding! In short, neither the mass media nor official sources may be very useful on this topic and greater

use of other secondary sources like books becomes more necessary.

Even where your project is based mainly on primary research, the use of published material can be extremely beneficial. For a start it can provide a context or background for your own piece of research, locating it in terms of wider issues or longer term trends. Hannah Gavron did this to good effect in her *Captive Wife* (1966). More specifically your own findings will be better understood or evaluated if they are compared to relevant data from other research.

As indicated above, it is not only sociological books that contain data of relevance to the sociological researcher. Consequently, some discussion of these other sources follows below. We also refer you back to the sections on the sociological perspective (pages 8-9), on social problem enquiries (pages 15-20) and on library usage (pages 29-33).

The question of subject boundaries is a complex one. On the one hand you need to remember that many related disciplines dealing with human behaviour do not stress the social dimension in the way sociology does. Psychology, for example, will stress individual factors in explaining human behaviour. Whilst such factors may be crucial they will not deal with the structural and historical forces which link the individual to society (see Mills 1970, pages 14-15). Equally the perspective of the lawyer or economist is quite different to that of the sociologist (Berger 1966, Chapter 2). Additionally, you need to be aware that subject boundaries are often matters of intense status and ideological dispute.

On the other hand, sociology itself has incorporated many non-sociologists into its fold. Consider the way the philosopher, G. H. Mead, influenced the development of symbolic interactionism or the ways the works and ideas of the psychiatrist, R. D. Laing, have become part of the sociology of the family. Media studies and cultural analyses are areas where sociology and other disciplines both converge and diverge.

The relationship between history and sociology is particularly interesting. History does not differ from sociology by virtue of its focus on the past; there can be sociological studies of the past and historians do write about current and recent events. One difference between the two is that history concentrates on particular or unique events or individual biographies, whilst sociology focuses on general issues, partly through its use of general concepts like class, gender, status and so on.

There is some truth in this; sociologists rarely study biographies in the way that historians do. The historian E. H. Carr (1975) strongly argues, however, that both subjects should concern themselves more with the relationship between the unique and general: 'the more sociological history becomes, and the more historical sociology becomes, the better for them both. Let the frontier between them be kept open for two-way traffic.'

An example of a sociological approach to the past is Young and Willmott's *Symmetrical Family* (1973), even if not all their arguments are convincing. An example of sociology using biography is Cashmore's study of *Black Sportsmen* (1982); in essence this is a case study approach.

In terms of your usage of history, it can be valuable for background material, for comparisons, a sense of social change, a search for explanations or causes, or even as a source of much of your main data. However, be guarded. Avoid too much specific detail or biography un-less it is shown to illustrate a general point - about class, social mobility or racism for example.

A further twist to this question of subject boundaries is raised by writings from within a feminist or Marxist perspective. Clearly there are many such writers who can readily be seen as operating within a largely sociological perspective. However, there are valuable contributions to our understanding made by sets of writers which cut across subject boundaries whether into philosophy or psychology, economics or political theory.

In short, there are many occasions when you may legitimately draw on social analyses or studies that don't belong in a narrow definition of sociology. However, when you do this, tread cautiously and be guided by your tutor.

There is another way in which books, perhaps especially non-sociological books, can provide useful data for your enquiry. This is in terms of Marwick's distinction between the witting and unwitting use of documents, as discussed in the Introduction to Part II. Much of the above discussion has been about the use of published material in terms of what its overt content is, what the author is intending to tell: the **witting** use of the book.

The **unwitting** use of books not only changes the way they are used but, in so doing, widens considerably the range of books that can be of sociological value to the research project. It enables non-sociological literature to be converted into sociological data.

This is perhaps best illustrated by a couple of examples and an exercise to work on. Looking again at the use of history books, but in a different way, you may be interested in ideology and curriculum or more loosely bias in the school system. Certainly, the recent conflict over what sort of history should be included in the national curriculum makes this an interesting issue.

With these or other possible themes, a study of history books in schools might be carried out to analyse how foreigner, other nations or British/English people are defined and represented. An interesting, impressionistic look at racism in US school books was made by Kozol (1968).

A similar example can be given by reference to an enquiry into sport. Leaving aside other research methods you may choose, you may decide to look at books for intending sports teachers at colleges of education. In these there may be practical guidance on many activities, but there may also, for example, be a section or chapter on the 'why?' of sport in school, ie its philosophy. Your research may be to explore what kind of philosophy or ideology of sport is being expressed: health; the importance of competitiveness; fun and variation in the school day; working as a team; the requirements of a fit workforce; the implementation of equal opportunities and so on. You may even find that the emphasis is related to the date the book was written or the social status of the schools being written about. The box on page 49 illustrates the way that sociological and non-sociological books can be used as sources of data or as topics in their own right; in short, both types of book can be used in the witting and unwitting sense.

Books as sources of ideas

Even if you are not directly using a book's findings as part of your own enquiry, there are many other ways that books can be of use to you in doing your research. We are here referring to the way sociological literature and published studies can give you ideas on how to plan and carry out this research. Other people's studies may suggest appropriate methods, indicate pitfalls or point to relevant concepts and theories to employ or issues to explore.

On a more practical level, if you're contemplating doing some observation or writing a questionnaire or interview schedule, it is essential to work out the issues you are interested in and the best ways to observe or ask about them. A published study can give considerable guidance on these

ACTIVITY 3 - MULTICULTURALISM

Other education books, such as set books in schools in various subjects, can be used as bases for data. For example, given the multicultural emphasis in the GCSE exam, how much of this is reflected in schools text books? If you have access to these texts still, attempt the following:

1. Define what you mean by multiculturalism.
2. List those subjects where you think multiculturalism is most readily expressed in teaching material like set books.
3. Take the remaining subjects and discuss why you think multiculturalism is not appropriate to them.
4. Look at the books in both lists to see in what ways, if any, multicultural themes are used.

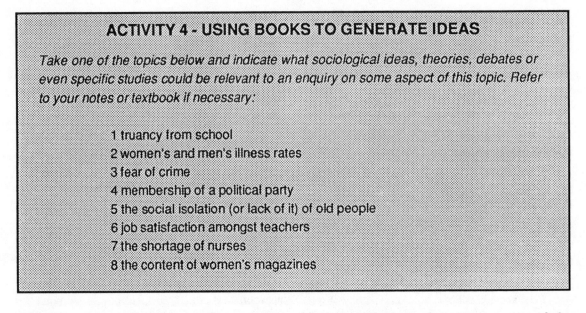

ACTIVITY 4 - USING BOOKS TO GENERATE IDEAS

Take one of the topics below and indicate what sociological ideas, theories, debates or even specific studies could be relevant to an enquiry on some aspect of this topic. Refer to your notes or textbook if necessary:

1 truancy from school
2 women's and men's illness rates
3 fear of crime
4 membership of a political party
5 the social isolation (or lack of it) of old people
6 job satisfaction amongst teachers
7 the shortage of nurses
8 the content of women's magazines

matters; indeed, as we mention earlier, you may decide it is appropriate to seek to replicate the approach or method of such a study.

This use of books points especially to the importance of doing some reading of relevant texts very early on in the planning of your research.

Below are some examples of the way a look at published sociological literature gave former A level students of ours guidance in doing their research projects.

Sociology of taxi drivers

A browse through the textbooks and in the library showed no evidence of published research for the student who chose this topic. This does not, of course, mean that no such studies had been carried out. However, the study of lorry drivers (Hollowell 1968) did provide some ideas that could be used and not just about how to terrorise cyclists. Rather it was the apparent individualism and the pursuit of autonomy at work that both occupations seemed to entail that proved a useful

conceptual starting point. An awareness of the literature on a given topic can also help with the operationalisation of a concept. For a general discussion of operationalising concepts, see pages 98-99 and McNeill (1990) pages 23-25.

Sociology of rock musicians

A mature student wanted to do his enquiry on being a rock musician; he had been involved in the pub-rock circuit in London for a number of years. Here the 1950s study of jazz musicians by Howard Becker (1963) was helpful. For example, it pointed to the way that apparently expressive work can have high levels of routinisation, partly because audiences often demand repetition of well known numbers.

Schools as 'total institutions'

Another student who had previously been at a boarding school (which he hated) read a study of life in a mental hospital (Goffman 1968b) for a detailed exploration of the concept of *total institu-*

DIFFERENT USES OF SOCIOLOGICAL AND NON-SOCIOLOGICAL BOOKS		
	Sociological books	**Non-sociological books**
As source	Burgoyne and Clarke (1983) 'Reconstituted Families'. This could be background reading for an enquiry on step parenting.	Paul Harrison's (1983) *Inside the Inner City* could provide useful case study data of a qualitative kind on any one of a variety of aspects of deprivation in Hackney or possibly any other inner city area. It's a valuable source of research ideas also. Written from the viewpoint of a critical social observer; it's a kind of extended investigative journalism.
As topic	All general sociology texts and those on the sociology of the family in your school or college library could be scanned (index etc) for references to domestic violence as part of an enquiry on the 'invisible crime' of wife battering or an enquiry into the feminist criticism of sociology as male-biased.	Children's stories - a local library or book shop could be asked for information on the most popular titles. These books could be analysed in terms of a range of sociological themes: images of national groups or foreigners; representations of the family; presentation of gender roles and so on. This could be accompanied by some theoretical discussion of these issues.

(i) These examples should be read in conjunction with those in the text.

(ii) Following our established usage, it is our contention that the use of books as sources of data is **secondary research** but, when they themselves are the topic under investigation, the research is **primary**.

tion in a largely retrospective study of his own school, supported by interviews with some current pupils. There are, of course, difficulties with retrospective studies, particularly the fallibility and selectivity of memory (see page 103).

Folk devils and moral panics

Stan Cohen's Mods and Rockers study (1972) is clearly an excellent starting point for many topics where the concepts of folk devils or moral panics might be applicable. Our students have used these in enquiries on surrogate motherhood, glue-sniffing and AIDS.

Guidelines on the use of books

In the above discussion we have indicated that some reference to books, or other publications, should be a feature of any enquiry you choose to do. We now suggest a number of points to bear in mind in the use of these books. Some of these are to do with being well-organised; others are more specific to how you can make the most of your reading and book usage.

Act early

If you need to order books, through the library inter-lending service, do so as early in your enquiry as possible; they can take a long time to come through. Keep a note of the date when they were ordered.

Be organised

Keep details of all the books that you use, however little use you have made of them; a card index is particularly useful for this (see pages 33-35). This is not only for your bibliography, but in case you need to refer back to them. The title, author, publisher and date should all be noted down. If it is a library book, you may wish to note which library and to make a note of the Dewey reference number. This could help you to locate the book again.

Take notes

If you are using a book at all, it is essential to take notes rather than rely, or try to rely, on memory. When you take notes, always record the source and page numbers.

The significance of a little

Remember that a book may be useful even if it only has a paragraph on your topic. Indeed, if your enquiry is heavily books-based and, if it is to be worthy of the term 'research', you cannot rely on one or two books telling you all you need to know about your topic. Sometimes the fact that your chosen topic has only a paragraph or a small section on it can be significant in its own right. It **may** indicate that the topic is marginalised or under-researched.

One of our students in the late 1970s wanted to do an enquiry on Afro-Caribbean women in Britain but found that very few of the books on race or immigration then available made any specific reference to them. Of course, the relative 'invisibility' of a topic can be interesting but it is also frustrating to the student researching it. In this case the candidate was able to make the enquiry a success by an excellent use of other research, including media analysis, and contacting black women's organisations.

Dates and datedness

Shipman (1988) reminds us that, 'There is always the possibility of redundancy in books and articles.' In other words, the situation they refer to may have changed so much by the time research is published that it can no longer be used as a reliable guide to the reality it claims to describe. He suggests a number of reasons for this including: the time taken to write it up, to publish it, to be summarised in other books and so on. Books then have a limited 'shelf-life' and 'syllabus-life' as recommended texts. He refers to Hargreaves' (1967) study of *Social Relations in a Secondary School* as one of the most influential British school studies, even in the 1980s, and yet the field work was carried out in one school in 1963-4 at a time when schooling was still selective.

There is no doubt that it is crucial to bear this in mind when referring to books and articles. To write as if the lifestyle of, say, Tunstall's (1962) Hull trawlermen had not changed in the last three decades, or as if the debate about gender inequality in the family could take place without some reference to domestic violence is to indicate a lack of understanding or effort on the part of the candidate - or both.

Nonetheless, books which were written a long time ago are not necessarily worthless, even to someone researching a recent phenomenon. Durkheim's study of suicide is still referred to, not really for its findings anymore, but as a landmark study in the development of sociology and as a good illustration of a certain methodological and theoretical orientation to the subject. Older studies can also be used as a basis for generating ideas or hypotheses for future research. Gavron, for example, cited earlier work on family life by Willmott and Young as an influence on the kinds of issues she sought to explore in her study.

Clearly, being up to date is more important if you are using the book as a source of witting data but less so if it's being used as unwitting data or as a source of ideas. To take one example of the latter, Stan Cohen's *Folk Devils and Moral Panics* is still useful for its concepts and general approach, despite the fact that some of these teenage rebels may now be grandparents.

Even in terms of books as sources of witting data, you and your marker have to keep a sense of proportion; it is unrealistic to expect the student to be up to date with forthcoming books, unpublished theses, recent articles in obscure journals and so on. Keeping an eye on the media can, of course, give scope for including topical issues or developments (see Chapter 4).

Bias in books

All the examining and validating bodies you are likely to be concerned with will expect you to treat the data you collect from books, or elsewhere, in a critical way. Information should not be taken at its face value.

It is one thing to say this, however, and another to act upon it. The process of evaluating material and detecting bias is made more difficult by the numbers of ways bias can enter into works. Many of these are dealt with in other sections, eg bias in interviews, samples, the media, government statistics and information from pressure groups. Below are a few observations on bias and criticism in relation to sociological books and articles.

- Can you find in other published works or reviews any criticisms of the book you are reading?
- Does the author make explicit their point of view? For example, a book may be written from an avowedly feminist viewpoint. Such books may be no more biased than others which have no such declared position; remember, many sociology books are sexist but few declare themselves to be such. Furthermore, this kind of bias need not indicate any suggestion of suppressed evidence or unsubstantiated claims. There are degrees and types of bias and you should not panic every time a piece of bias is discovered. Part of the bias of feminism is to research topics previously not addressed by male sociology, eg Oakley's (1976) study of housework. In some ways then, feminism (or other critical ideologies like Marxism) are double-edged as regards bias. On the one hand they are selecting topics and researching them in such a way as to highlight

gender (or class inequality) and some say they go too far; on the other hand they may be pointing to a bias towards understating these inequalities in mainstream sociology.

- Following up this point, you may detect bias in the language an author uses, such as whether it is male (use of 'mankind') or gender neutral ('humanity'). The significance of this may only be in the date it was written; thus Shipman's (1988) 3rd edition of his book on social research states: 'Across the two editions of this book the continual reference to "he" and "his" has been dropped. Even more important, the first edition in 1972 never considered the sexist bias in the evidence considered.'

- What assumptions would you make about a writer who made frequent references to class, the State and capitalism or, alternatively, made regular use of phrases like 'society's norms and values' or 'society's needs'?

- Bias by omission has already been referred to several times and feminism is a valuable sensitising perspective here as is an awareness of race/ethnicity as major variables in modern Britain. Thus, any discussions of inequality, for example, in a book you are reading about modern Britain, is inadequate if it makes no reference to gender or race; this applies to educational opportunity, health, old age, poverty etc.

- You may not be able to put your finger on why something seems biased but still feel that it is. Try to examine your reaction and impression. It could be that it is not a specific ideological bias as such but just a feature of the sociological perspective as outlined by Berger (1966):

'To ask sociological questions, then, presupposes that one is interested in looking some distance beyond the commonly accepted or officially defined goals of human actions...It may even presuppose a measure of suspicion about the way in which human events are officially interpreted by the authorities, be they political, juridical or religious in character.'

- Because distancing oneself from the authorities is sometimes thought of as left-wing, this could misdirect evaluation. Berger also refers to the sociology of knowledge and, drawing on Schütz's concept of the taken-for-granted world, indicates how people inhabit a world of assumptions that derive from their place in society and history. People may hold taken-for-granted views about a whole range of issues from masculinity to the monarchy, from food to 'foreigners'. Many of these beliefs will remain implicit, validated by the others in their social world but seldom explored or challenged. Berger argues that people who 'like the safety of the rules and the maxims of...the world-taken-for-granted, should stay away from sociology.' His style is rather superior but it could well be that, some of the time when people detect bias in sociology, what they are discovering is their reaction to holding cherished beliefs and institutions up for analysis.

There are other forms of bias than those just discussed and other forms of evaluation than detecting bias. Many of these are discussed in relation to the other sources and methods discussed. Generally, the more familiar you are with sociology, through reading, exercises etc, the better your evaluation should become.

Bear in mind that some bias is inevitable, if only because studies reflect certain ideas about what issues are important to research. This is what is meant by 'perspective': a way of looking at the world. Furthermore bias doesn't invalidate a study and you shouldn't therefore get too carried away if you discover a value-laden word in the text of a book. Nonetheless, the bias has to be taken account of in interpreting and evaluating the text.

Secondly, not all perspectives are of equal sociological value; to employ a metaphor of Carr (1964) a mountain may be viewed differently from a variety of positions but some perspectives give a clearer idea of the mountain's size or shape than other perspectives do. In short, try to evaluate the study **and** its theoretical background or assumptions.

Using books

4

Using the media

Whatever your chosen topic it is possible that at some stage in your study you will use information from the mass media. We have already discussed how any material for your enquiry may be used either as a **resource** or as a **topic** (see the Introduction to Part II). Thus, there are broadly two sorts of uses that you might make of the media in your project.

One is as a source of information. Media reports of public debates, summaries of official and unofficial reports, and articles representing different points of view are often invaluable in providing background detail. Here you are using the media as a data bank of facts and opinions.

But, on occasion, analysing the media may be a more central concern of your study. For example, you may be studying a moral panic, looking at the representation in the media of certain groups or the social construction of news issues. In these examples the media and their processes become the object of your study. You will probably be concerned with issues of distortion, bias, representation and ideology.

Media information

In this chapter we are using a broad definition of the media which includes fiction and entertainment as well as news and comment. Social issues such as rape, homelessness, divorce, disability and addiction are often dealt with in fictional forms such as films and television plays.

Once you have made your choice, look out for plays, films etc as they can often give you useful leads. The treatment of a topic such as homosexuality in comedy programmes or soap operas may give you as many useful insights as a 'serious' discussion or documentary programmes.

Beyond the obvious forms of mass media: newspapers, radio and television, film, magazines and books and so on, there are many minor publications with narrow and specialist audiences (see box on page 56) which can be very useful. Unlike mass media, these may be harder to track down. Consult *Willings Press Guide*, the *Directory of Pressure Groups* and even classified telephone directories in your local library for help. This should be done in the early stages of your research. Once you have located them, these specialist media can be a mine of useful information and may give you contacts for interviews and other useful sources.

One advantage of using media information is that it's easy to collect. A professional sociologist may spend hours coaxing information from respondents in interview and weeks gaining their confidence in observation situations.

By contrast, the mass media are a very convenient source of information. They are cheap and easily available. They don't use technical language

SOME IDEAS FOR SPECIALIST MEDIA	
Specialist magazines	
Politics and current affairs periodicals *(New Statesman and Society, The Listener, Economist, Spectator, Marxism Today, Social Studies Review).*	Broad, though often partisan, coverage of social issues. Worth scanning regularly. Use library for index of articles and back numbers.
Women's magazines, ethnic minority press, gay newspapers, hobby and leisure interest magazines, teenage magazines and children's comics etc.	There's an enormous range of these. Relevance depends on your choice of topic. Be alert to the 'committed' position of some of these.
In-house journals and newsletters	Produced by most medium to large organisations (pressure groups, companies, trade unions, professional associations, religious organisations, hospitals etc). Usually will not be found on newsagents' shelves. Direct approach to the organisation necessary.
Promotional videos and literature	Brochures, leaflets and other public relations information available from many organisations. A particularly useful example is the Open University catalogue of literature including broadcasts.

and they are often the only source of up to date information.

This last point is particularly appropriate if you are studying contemporary events. Sociological studies often take months or years to reach publication. If your study is about a topical issue, the media may be your main source of information.

Using media information

While it may be relatively easy to collect a considerable folder of press cuttings on your topic, using this material effectively requires some thought and effort.

Whenever you use secondary sources the examiners will be looking to see that you have made some effort to analyse and evaluate the material. In presenting media information, therefore, you should show that you are aware of possible sources of bias and distortion, and omissions.

The evaluation of evidence is always a tricky judgement to make and it's difficult to set rigid guidelines. When using material from newspapers you should consider the political allegiances of the paper. These will be most prominent in editorial comments and many papers try to separate reporting from editorial comment. Moreover, papers often publish signed articles by writers whose views differ from their own. You cannot assume, for example, that the *Daily Telegraph* will only give space to Conservative ideas.

There are many other influences which may affect what a newspaper prints. Newspaper proprietors may occasionally influence editorial policy. Recently, for example, newspapers owned by one media magnate have been accused of giving excessive coverage to the launch of his satellite TV station. Legal or state security constraints may apply to certain topics, and journalistic 'news values' - dramatic events, famous personalities, human interest stories etc - will influence the se-

lection, placement and construction of news (see Barrat 1986).

It's not that you can 'never trust what the media say', but you should be cautious in your use of media information. If you are unsure of an item, try to find corroborating evidence from another source. You might consult *Social Trends* and the *British Crime Survey* to check a media claim of rising crime rates, bearing in mind, of course, that official statistics have their own shortcomings (see Chapter 5). Your tutor will probably also advise if you are doubtful.

You should be cautious when using any secondary data which, by definition, has been collected for other, usually non-sociological, purposes. The issues and questions which you might wish to raise in your enquiry may differ from the

---

ACTIVITY 5 - BRAINSTORMING MEDIA USES IN ENQUIRIES

This could be an individual or a class activity. Look at the following titles and then brainstorm the different ways the media could be useful in developing the enquiry topic. Make a list of particular journals, programmes or publicity from organisations that could be of use and suggest other ways in which the media could be analysed:

'An examination of how society treats and perceives "Heavy Metal" fans'
'A study of bullying in schools - a comparison between a primary and secondary school'
'A study of arranged marriages in North Cyprus and London'
'A sociological investigation into women's drinking habits'

Remember our broad distinction between two possible uses of the media: as a source of information and as a topic in their own right and try to find, where relevant, examples of both. On the first topic you might take press reports of the **numbers** of fans arrested at a heavy metal concert as **information** on the perception of this group by social control agencies. Or you might turn your focus to the **media treatment** of heavy metal music fans as an indication of how they are treated and perceived by society.

(This list was selected from actual AS enquiry titles submitted to the London Board)

concerns of the media. You will also need to be alert to the chance that some themes or perspectives may never be considered. Always cite the source of your information, date of publication and bring up any misgivings you have about the information.

You can expect the specialist media to be more openly partisan and one-sided than the mass media. For instance, a promotional video for university or polytechnic is unlikely to spend much time discussing student drop-out, poor facilities or low pass rates. In the same way, the journal of the Police Federation and *West Indian World* can be expected to have very different views on the causes of crime and the extent of police corruption reflecting their particular ideologies and world views.

This is not a problem as long as you are clear about who is writing, what audience it is aimed at, and which points of view are likely to be stressed or left out. In fact, as we discuss next, the biases and distortions of the media can be a revealing source of information in their own right.

Media analysis

Next we look at some strategies for examining the media in more detail. You may not need to use these unless an analysis of some aspect of the media plays a large part in your project. But if you want to do your own research into how gender relations are portrayed in teenage fiction, for example, or how the media reports a particular event or social problem then you'll need a systematic approach.

Content analysis

In addition to their more familiar repertoire of research methods sociologists have developed new tools to study the media. One of the first approaches was content analysis. This is a quantitative method - chiefly a counting exercise which addresses questions of how many, how often, and how much?

The purpose of content analysis is to produce an objective record of the frequency of pre-selected items which the researcher is interested in. A superficial example could be counting 'swearing' or 'acts of violence' on television (both have been done) in order to back up a claim of 'declining standards'. As a method it shares something in common with the questionnaire - and is subject to similar criticisms from anti-positivists. It remains, however, a useful means of drawing generalisations about the media when used appropriately.

You may already have come across this approach in your sociology course. Golding and Middleton's (1982) research into press images of welfare claimants and the Glasgow University Media Group's (GUMG) study in 1976 of the television representation of industrial disputes are good examples.

Scale, selection and sampling

It is vital that you do not set yourself goals which are too ambitious. Content analysis is a laborious and time-consuming process, at times even the professionals get it wrong.

The GUMG, for example, set out to videotape and analyse all television news programmes that were broadcast in one year. In the event, they generated so much material that they were forced to limit the period of study to six months and it was several years before they were ready to publish their final analysis. They were a team of eight professional sociologists; remember you're on your own.

CONTENT ANALYSIS CATEGORIES - ROLES IN CHILDREN'S BOOKS

The content of the children's roles

The sex for which the role was prescribed	Toys and pets	Activities	Taking the lead in both sex activities	Learning a new skill	The adult roles presented
GIRLS ONLY	1 Doll 2 Skipping rope 3 Doll's pram	1 Preparing the tea 2 Playing with dolls 3 Taking care of younger siblings	1 Hopping 2 Shopping with parents 3 Skipping	1 Taking care of younger siblings	1 Mother 2 Aunt 3 Grand-mother
BOYS ONLY	1 Car 2 Train 3 Aeroplane 4 Boat 5 Football	1 Playing with cars 2 Playing with trains 3 Playing football 4 Lifting or pulling heavy objects 5 Playing cricket 6 Watching adult males in occupational roles 7 Heavy gardening	1 Going exploring 2 Climbing trees 3 Building things 4 Taking care of pets 5 Sailing boats 6 Flying kites 7 Washing and polishing Dad's car	1 Taking care of pets 2 Making or build-ing 3 Saving or res-cuing people or pets 4 Playing sports	1 Father 2 Uncle 3 Grandfather 4 Postman 5 Farmer 6 Fisherman 7 Shop or business owner 8 Policeman 9 Builder 10 Bus driver 11 Bus con-ductor 12 Train driver 13 Railway porter
BOTH SEXES	1 Book 2 Ball 3 Paints 4 Bucket and spade 5 Dog 6 Cat 7 Shop	1 Playing with pets 2 Writing 3 Reading 4 Going to the seaside 5 Going on a fam-ily outing	_	_	1 Teacher 2 Shop assis-tant

(i) Taken from Lobban's (1974) analysis of children's reading schemes.
(ii) This gives you an example of the sorts of categories used in content analysis. Lobban would have produced also a set of precise definitions of each category to avoid confusion/overlap. Eg is 'going to the seaside' also to be counted under 'going on a family outing'? (see 'categorising and counting' pages 61-62)

Inevitably your resources will be much more modest. You may, for example, examine all the newspaper reports for one day of a particular event. This works well if the item you choose is newsworthy and covered by all papers. Major events such as the Hillsborough football stadium disaster are well suited to this approach. In the nature of things such events are unpredictable and this creates problems in planning your study.

Another approach is to be more selective and collect reports from two or three different media on the assumption that their approaches will be representative of others. Looking at the press alone, you might find it useful to categorise them into 'popular' papers (eg *Sun, Mirror, Star*), 'middlebrow' papers (eg *Mail, Express, Today*) and 'quality' papers (eg *Guardian, Telegraph, Independent, Times*). You could then choose one paper to represent each category and limit your comparisons in this way.

Much will depend on the objectives of your study. For some purposes it may be more appropriate to group papers according to their political persuasion or, perhaps, their ownership (Murdoch vs Maxwell etc.).

Alternatively you may compare different examples within the same genre - for example the contrasting views of police work represented in, say, *The Bill* and *Miami Vice*. In this case it would probably be sufficient to work on a sample of programmes from each series. You could count and compare:

- the gender or ethnic composition of police officers depicted;
- the numbers of black/female officers in senior positions;
- 'types' of offences;

- the typical social characteristics (age, gender, race etc) of the 'TV villain' - compared with published crime statistics.

The scale of any such study would have to be limited. Therefore, it is essential that you are clear about what your aims are. Be prepared to justify your choice of media when you present your findings. Avoid making unsupported generalisations from small samples of the sort: 'All British police series are...'.

You won't be penalised for setting yourself modest goals so long as you show that you are aware of the limitations of your findings. Here, as elsewhere in your project, you are not expected to produce the definitive work on a topic but rather to show that you can handle sociological methods in a small scale study and reflect sensibly on your findings. Remember that even the most ambitious sociological study has to set itself some boundaries.

Resources

Current copies of written media are usually readily available, although if you have to buy a number of editions your research costs will rapidly escalate. Finding people willing to pass on old copies is one solution. Your school, college or local library may help. Some libraries keep press cuttings on selected issues, others will allow you access to back-copies although photocopying can become expensive.

Smaller libraries do not have the resources to hold back-copies of newspapers for long. Major public reference libraries will hold larger stocks of back-copies of papers and periodicals although you may need to obtain a letter of introduction from your tutor to gain access to these.

Studying broadcasts as they are transmitted is a formidable task and audio or video tape-recording is a very useful aid. You may be able to get programme scripts by writing to the programme director but don't bank on this. Again, don't amass more material than you can comfortably handle.

Categorising and counting

Once you have chosen your media sample, the work of analysis begins. The first stage in this is to choose a set of categories relevant to your aims. Your choice of categories for content analysis will be guided by the original project aims. Existing sociological literature can give you a starting point. You might try to update some of the findings of a study, produce evidence relevant to a sociological controversy or apply the conclusions of a study to other areas of the media.

Developing an appropriate set of categories is not a simple process and to some extent you will have to proceed by trial and error. It's essential that you carry out a dummy run using the categories because you will inevitably find overlaps and items that cannot easily be placed into your system. This 'piloting' of the categories allows you to refine and improve them before you start the analysis in earnest.

Once you have a notion of the sorts of ideas you want to examine, produce some loose hypotheses. You might, for instance, decide to compare the treatment of 'aliens' in space fiction comics with the role of the 'foreigner' in British society, or compare gender relations in women's magazine fiction of the 1990s with that of the 1960s or another time period; you may attempt to describe the ways in which young Asian men are treated in the Press.

Whatever your interest, and there are many possibilities for research here, you should then begin to look at examples of the media you intend to study to see whether there is enough relevant data to process. You will also need to develop tight definitions of your categories so that you can classify media items accordingly.

In this pilot stage of the research you have to be flexible. Be prepared to modify, re-define, add to, subdivide and combine categories in the light of what you find until you have a version that works with the small sample of media texts that you have been working with.

Inevitably, when you begin the main analysis, you will find items that present you with categorisation problems. This is unavoidable, just as a respondent may give an unexpected response to a pre-coded questionnaire which cannot be slotted into one of the pre-defined response categories. You will have to develop ground rules to deal with these obstinate cases and apply them consistently throught your analysis. Don't change your categories halfway through unless you are able to go back and re-analyse, with the new categories, all the material you have already processed.

It is very important to keep an 'open mind' when doing your analysis. Don't look only for those examples that support your preconceptions. It's as important to know that you were wrong about something as to find that you were right. The temptation to find what you want to find is a constant and inherent pitfall in this and many other types of research.

The data of content analysis only becomes informative when you begin to make comparisons. To take a simple example, the finding that on a particular day the *Sun* newspaper has, say, three pages on the 'Royal Family' does not, on its own, tell us very much. Such absolute statistics reveal much more when compared with other data. For example, 'What proportion are these three pages of the entire paper: 5%, 10%?', 'Is this percentage the same in other editions of the same title?', 'How does this compare with the coverage of the Royal Family in other newspapers or broadcast news?'

The repetitive and uninspiring task of measuring space or time allocation with ruler and/or stop watch can, nevertheless, produce interesting results. Another dimension of news analysis is to compare news priorities. 'Where does the story appear?', 'Is it front page news or the first item in a broadcast or is it relegated to a lower priority in the media text?' ('text' is the term used by media researchers to refer to a media product such as a newspaper, film, or television programme. Despite the term, it does not have to be in written format). Such questions allow you to contrast different media and to find differences and similarities in their news values.

A third, common dimension of content analysis is frequency. For instance, 'How often are men shown doing domestic tasks in magazine advertisements?', 'How often is Asian family life depicted as a scene of conflict in soap-operas?' Again, in order to make sense of answers to such questions some comparative material is necessary.

Frequency is not, of course, the whole story. You may recall a TV advertisement for *Persil* washing powder in which a young man accidentally spills the powder on the floor while trying to wash a shirt. Although this was a case of a man doing a domestic task it was not clear evidence of 'role reversal'; why was he only washing his own clothes? Why was he shown as so incompetent? Was this **really** a challenge to gender ideologies?

Presenting results

So far we have focused on comparisons within and between different media. Fruitful comparisons can also be made with other data. 'Is divorce more common in TV drama than "real life"?' - comparison with official divorce rates might be interesting here. In their study, the Glasgow University Media Group found that TV news highlighted disputes in the motor industry although in official figures for the same period other industrial sectors appeared more 'strike-prone'.

You could also endeavour to put your findings in the context of exisiting sociological studies or the results of your own primary research. Jock Young (1971) employed the latter approach in his comparison of media images of young marihuana users with the results of his own participant observation with such groups.

As you will be dealing with quantitative data you will need to use simple tables or charts to display the results effectively (see Chapter 9).

Evaluating your content analysis

The purpose of evaluation is to show that you are informed about the strengths and weaknesses of your analysis and can interpret your findings.

Explain your choice of media and discuss how representative your sample is. It's a good idea to consider here how your study could be improved or extended, or what further work could be done to improve the quality of your evidence. You should also describe the system of categories developed for the study and reflect on problems of categorisation that occurred during the study.

Content analysis, by its nature, lifts the particular items you are studying out of the context of the media text. It is a technique for appraising a range of media from a broad perspective. Inevitably some detail and meaning is lost in this process. You should show that you are conscious of the possible distortions that may be produced by considering items out of context.

Finally you must try to connect your results to existing research findings making use of sociological theory and concepts.

Language and image

Close analysis of a specific media text can also be a very useful form of analysis. It's often a good idea to juxtapose the broad sweep of a quantitative analysis with a detailed exploration of one or two texts.

Analysing language and image requires quite a different set of skills from that of content analysis. You're more concerned with **how** things are presented than with **what** is presented and you will be on the look-out for subtle shades of meaning which may be deeply embedded in the text and require some effort to dig out. You should be alert to the fact that journalists, camera operators, editors and producers **always have a choice** over which word or phrase to use or which camera angle to select. The question is: 'Why did they choose this one?'

For instance, quite different meanings are conveyed by 'terrorist', 'urban guerrilla' and 'freedom fighter' although, on the surface, they may appear to be simply factual descriptions. Similarly, the GUMG found that while trade unionists were described, in TV news, aggressively making 'demands', employers more reasonably made 'offers'.

A recent example of this more qualitative approach is Anne Karpf's (1988) study of the representation of medical matters in the media. One section of the study examines medical dramas in film and television. Karpf's review takes in 50 years of film and television production to highlight various themes and trends in medical drama. Given the scale of the exercise, it was clearly impossible to carry out a large scale quantitative analysis - although she refers to quantitative studies by other authors to illustrate, for example, the popularity of the medical genre (eg Gerbner's (1982) finding that health professionals outnumber other professionals by a ratio of five to one in American prime time television).

Instead, she shows how the images of medicine in programmes such as the early *Emergency Ward 10* and *Dr Kildare*, or *Marcus Welby MD*, *Casualty*, and *St Elsewhere* both construct and reflect widely held views of medicine. She examines the roles of doctors (usually male and heroic), nurses (nearly always female), 'geysers of nurturance and intuitive mothers to the world' and ancillary workers (porters, cleaning staff etc) largely absent except in more recent productions.

The image of medicine that is put together in medical drama is considerably distorted and, according to Karpf, ideological. A TV doctor rarely makes mistakes, is primarily concerned with the patient as a whole person, always has time to listen to problems, and is a supreme technical wizard. Karpf contrasts this image of the 'benign curer' with studies which show that patients often perceive doctors to be insensitive to their feelings.

Karpf links the kindly image of TV medicine of the 1960s to a desire to offer a reassuring view of state medicine, which had been rapidly expanding in the post war period. She quotes Anthony Kearey, producer of the British TV series *Emergency Ward 10*: 'We wanted to overcome the pre-war attitude of the British public of hospitals as institutions, places to be avoided at all costs. We wanted people to respond to new research in medicine.' The father-figure role of many early screen doctors was also a reassertion of traditional patriarchal values. In the 1960s and 1970s: 'There was widespread concern about the rising rates of divorce, and the effects of the growth in women's employment...As the white male tele-doctor made good the damage and healed the hurt, the doctor shows offered reassurance that the system could succour and patriarchy provide' (Karpf 1988).

One prerequisite of such research is access to a range of media texts old and new. But you might be able to do a similar type of study of the changing styles of police series or cookery programmes, perhaps renting old videos. If you are keen, the *British Film Institute* in London may be willing to help you with access to archive film and television material.

CHECKLIST - USING THE MEDIA

 Have you kept a careful eye open for any **references to your topic in the media**?

 Do you know what **'specialist media'** there are which could be helpful to you in your enquiry?

 Are the media references best used as **sources** of information or as **topics** to be analysed in their own right?

 If the media references are to be used as sources of information, have you considered the issue of **bias** (eg by checking statistics quoted in a radio programme against other sources)?

 If the media references are to be used as topics (eg studying the media treatment of an issue) is a **quantitative approach** (content analysis) or a **qualitative approach** (language and image analysis) more appropriate?

 In what ways would it be useful to **compare your analysis with the findings of other research**?

5

Statistical sources

Statistics - official and unofficial

Modern societies, said Max Weber, are increasingly bureaucratic. One aspect of bureaucratic organisation is the keeping of written (now electronically stored?) records, including statistical records on citizens, clients, customers and so on. Many of these organisations are private, business or voluntary associations, for example. Many of them are official or semi-official, either departments of government at central or local levels or organisations partly or wholly financed or set up by government, such as the *Commission for Racial Equality* or the *Sports Council*.

The boundary between official and unofficial organisations is not absolute. For example, recent privatisations of previously publicly owned industries has meant that organisations like *British Gas* or *British Telecom* are now private rather than public or official organisations. There is even talk of privatising organisations of more obvious sociological interest, like prisons. This has not only changed the official definition of these as statistical sources but it could influence what statistics are collected, how they are collated and whether or not they are made publicly accessible.

Sociology and statistical sources

It is important to note from the outset that organisations have a variety of motives for the collection and possible publication of these data: commercial, political, managerial, administrative, social control, public relations and so on. Consequently, whilst you may find much data relevant to your study, there are likely to be many questions of sociological interest that are not explored in this gathering of statistical data. Indeed, the sociologist is not only likely to find these statistics partial in their coverage but biased in a more systematic way as well. This does not mean that they cannot be used but they do need to be used with care, preferably in conjunction with data from other sources. Sometimes, it is the bias in the statistics that you are interested in.

There are times when official sources of statistics can be very useful to the sociologist doing a research project; figures for gas supply cut-offs for non-payment of bills could be relevant to a study of poverty, for example. Generally, however, it is statistics kept by government agencies, especially the government itself, which are likely to be the biggest source of recorded statistical data relevant to your enquiry.

The rest of this chapter largely concentrates on outlining some of the main sources and possible uses of various kinds of statistical data, mostly from official sources. However, before beginning this discussion, a more general observation regarding the sociological use of official statistics is called for.

This observation concerns the fact that, from the 1960s onwards, there was a widespread, but not universal, reaction against measurement or quantification in sociology. This anti-positivism was exemplified by criticism of Durkheim's reliance on official statistics in his study of suicide (1970) and a more general critique of official statistics in criminology. There was a tendency in some quarters to reject numbers, especially from official sources, as at best irrelevant to the pursuit of good sociology. In our view this was an over reaction and these statistics can be used to good effect by the professional and student sociologist alike. This view, increasingly common in sociology generally, does not necessarily imply any acceptance of a positivistic model of social science. (It could be noted in passing, however, that one of the main sources indicating the extent of the under-reporting of crime in official statistics is an officially funded, large scale statistical survey - the *British Crime Survey*.)

The sources and availability of statistics

The main sources of statistics are likely to be contained in the large volumes of data published by *Her Majesty's Stationery Office* (HMSO); these are outlined below on pages 69-70.

However, it is important to note that the potential range of sources is very wide indeed, particularly if unofficial sources are included as well. A list of all such possible sources is impossible since the number and range of agencies that produce statistics potentially relevant to a sociological enquiry increases with each different topic chosen. The enormous number of private organisations producing statistics for public consumption is suggested by the fact that most large organisations have a public relations or education section; smaller organisations often belong to trade or group associations that have similar departments.

Quite often, private organisations provide the government with statistical returns which are then reproduced in official publications: the Football League (on match attendances); private medical companies (on numbers of subscribers, persons insured etc); youth groups, like Guides (membership figures).

Conversely, many organisations, including charities and pressure groups, supplement their own data with statistics based on their own selection and analysis of official statistics. These can be very useful sources of information and we refer you to the *Directory of Pressure Groups*, *Directory of British Associations* or the *Charities Digest*. Some more general issues concerning unofficial sources of data are raised in the chapter on documents.

As Slattery (1986) notes, in his very useful account of official statistics, the government obtains its own statistical data in two main ways:

State records

The Registrar of Birth, Deaths and Marriages, the Inland Revenue, the Home Office, the Departments of Health, Social Security, Education, Employment, Environment and so on - all these central government agencies regularly collect data on all people born, living or dying in the United Kingdom. This data is not all of the same status; birth statistics are an almost completely accurate measure of what they claim to be measuring, whereas Inland Revenue returns are not!

Don't forget that the local council does much statistical gathering as well, so does your school or college. You may be able to obtain and use this more local information in conjunction with other research techniques, including some kind of primary research.

Surveys of the population

The largest of these is the ten-yearly survey of every household in the country - the *Census*. Not only is it national but it is compulsory as well; consequently its coverage of the population is exceptionally comprehensive.

In addition, there are sample surveys, often involving larger samples than academic researchers can afford. The main ones are the *Family Expenditure Survey*, the *General Household Survey*, the *Labour Force Survey,* and the recently added *British Crime Survey* (see McNeill's (1988) very useful interview with one of these researchers, Pat Mayhew, about some of the methodological issues involved, *New Statesman and Society* 9-12-1988). There are other surveys carried out by or for the government on issues which may be of relevance to you depending on your choice of topic; Slattery provides a list of many of these.

Like the *Census* itself, most of the sample surveys are concerned with factual data - employment, household composition, possession of consumer durables etc - but there is also the partly government financed *British Social Attitudes Survey*. This is certainly worth consultation; see page 70 for details.

The above methods are how the government obtains its information. From the public's point of view these data are made available on a wide range of publications from HMSO. These can be bought direct from HMSO or other booksellers, but it is far better to use a reference library. Some are so useful that your school or college should be persuaded to buy copies of their own.

Before outlining these publications more fully, we would like to urge those of you easily put off by statistics not to be so. A whole book of tables can be daunting, but a careful look at the contents page could guide you quickly to the most useful parts. Secondly, do note that much can be obtained from a table or graph without doing any sophisticated statistical or mathematical analysis.

As regards the official publications themselves, the *HMSO Statistics Catalogue 1990* gives an extremely valuable list of available books and sources; it's free and well worth having. Here we select and outline some of those most likely to be of relevance to you. Where we feel it useful for your school or college library to have a copy of their own, we have indicated the price.

At the general level, the catalogue itself recommends *Guide to Official Statistics No. 5* which outlines the official and some unofficial publications that can or should be referred to on subjects as diverse as the weather and policing. It refers to regular as well as ad hoc and occasional publications. From your point of view, the briefer discussion in *Key Data* (see page 69) is likely to be perfectly adequate if you need to pursue some source of data.

In addition to these there are many more specialist publications that may be of relevance, depending on your choice of topic. Here is a selection to give you a sense of the range available: *Smoking Among Secondary School Children in 1988; Informal Carers; Women's Migration; Marriage, Fertility and Divorce; Social Security Statistics 1989.*

Apart from these government publications

UK OFFICIAL STATISTICS - MAIN PUBLICATIONS

1. *Social Trends*

Annual. The most important source for social scientists. Currently £21.95. (See comment on page 75.)

Deals with a wealth of topics on population, household size and composition, divorce, employment, income and wealth, health and social services etc.

2. *Key Data*

Annual. Published since 1986. Cheap - currently £3.50. Definitely worth school/college buying a copy.

A range of data selected from the larger publications. Coverage includes demography, family and household, employment, law, leisure, housing etc. It also includes a section on *Government Statistics - a brief guide to sources.*

3. *Britain 1990 - An Official Handbook*

Note that official versions of social reality may not correspond with sociological versions (see pages 8, 75 and Berger 1966, chapter 2).

This goes well beyond social issues into geography, economics, climate and so on. It is still worth using both as a sociological resource and perhaps as a topic as well (see pages 41-43).

4. *The General Household Survey*

Latest edition, currently 1987. Based on a large scale (15,000) sample survey. Very useful - currently £13.90.

Includes questions on population and households etc to fill in the gaps between the ten-yearly censuses. Also includes questions on other topics eg share ownership, cultural activities etc.

5. *Family Expenditure Survey*

Annual. Based on a large representative sample of households. Currently £18.00.

Deals with aspects of family income and expenditure, including items such as food, clothing, alcohol, tobacco and leisure.

6. *Labour Force Survey*

1987 edition - out of print, new edition due May 1990.

Part of the European Community wide statistical gathering exercise on many economic and social aspects of these societies.

(continued next page)

7. *Annual Abstract Of Statistics*

Less useful than *Social Trends* as it covers so many non-social topics.	Very comprehensive, deals with a wide range of matters, including issues like law, family life etc but also much that is non-sociological. Unlike *Social Trends*, this volume contains only tables with no discussion.

8. *Regional Trends*

Annual (see also *Key Statistics for Urban Areas 1981* on every town over 20,000; 4 volumes - the North; South-West and Wales; Midlands; South-East).	Useful for comparative or more specialised data about Britain, such as education (eg school leavers' exam results); health (eg cervical smear tests or diet); demography, income, employment and so on.

9. *Monthly Digest of Statistics*

Rarely are such up-to-date figures necessary; indeed they can be misleading - 'one swallow does not make a summer.' However the data does cover the previous two years.	Could be useful if you're researching patterns of employment/unemployment. Much of the data oriented towards economic and business issues.

10. *Criminal Statistics*

Annual. November 1989 edition £16.00.	Looks at rates of recorded crime including types, category of offender (age/gender), punishment and sentencing patterns; differences by police region and so on.

11. *British Crime Survey*

1989 edition (third so far) £10. Very useful.	Incorporates a victim survey and patterns of/reasons for reporting/non-reporting; fear of crime; patterns of victimisation (including recently on racial attacks) etc.

12. *Education Statistics for the UK*

	Includes data on finance, staffing and curriculum, qualifications, higher education etc.

13. *British Social Attitudes*

Partly officially funded.	Covers attitudes to religion, sexuality, education politics and other topics.

there are the selections from and commentaries on these statistics found in academic works. For example the books on class and sex differences in Britain (Reid 1981; Reid and Wormald 1982) draw on such data. One of the most useful is the collection of statistical analyses of British society this century and especially since World War II (Halsey 1988). It draws on official and academic research and incorporates commentary on statistical sources; a highly valuable source book for the library.

The uses of official statistics

Earlier in the book (pages 41-43) we distinguished between using a source as a resource or as a topic. This witting and unwitting usage of sources like books or newspapers applies also to official statistics. The witting usage is the more obvious and gives the widest range of reasons for using official statistics. However, there may be good reasons for looking at official statistics themselves in terms of what issues are asked about or omitted, what ways information is categorised and so on. In this sense you may combine both approaches in your inter-

---

INTERNATIONAL STATISTICS - SOME SOURCES

With 1992 in mind, or more generally perhaps, those enquiries with an international or comparative element, the following publications have been selected:

1. *Europe in Figures* 1989/90 edition.	Derived from *Eurostat*, the European Statistical Office of the member countries of the European Community. Is relevant to sociology - and to geography, economics etc.
2. *UNESCO Statistical Yearbook 1989* Based on over 200 countries and territories.	Looks both at education issues like literacy and levels of expenditure and at more general cultural/media issues: book production, museums etc.
3. *1988 World Health Statistics* Annual. Based on over 200 countries and territories.	Health and demographic data from around the globe, including comparative mortality rates, causes of death and so on.
4. *World Statistics in Brief* Annual. Basic information in a concise publication.	Particularly relevant to issues of development, includes data on education, demography, health, economics etc for a wide range of countries.

These titles can all be obtained from HMSO which acts as the UK sales agent for a variety of international organisations, such as the United Nations, European Community, World Health Organisation

pretation, analysis and evaluation of official statistics.

The following examples should illustrate these ideas more fully.

Official statistics as sources

- *As background information* - this may simply mean giving some national or historical figures which provide broader framework as the context for a more focused enquiry. Eg an enquiry on 'Community Care for the Elderly' would benefit from some demographic data on the growth of the elderly population.
- *To compare or contrast with your research findings* - as part of the study on 'Gender and Academic Choice' you may have carried out a count of male/female ratios in a range of subjects at a local school. Your findings could be matched against national figures for entrants at GCSE and/or A level - any differences could be the basis of further research or explanation.
- *For data that's otherwise difficult to obtain* - this might include patterns of household structure, trends in home ownership, participation in sport, death rates etc.
- *Charting long term trends* - this could be linked to the analysis of related events and processes (laws, wars, technological or economic change etc). Take great care if you are attempting before and after analysis. One reason for caution in this kind of analysis is the temptation to see associations or changes of pattern as a result of a direct causal influence between the variables being analysed. Changes can be the result of other, perhaps unknown, factors or even be coincidental. For example, in the 1950s both lung cancer and car exhaust emissions were rising and there was some suggestion that

the latter caused the former; we now know that tobacco was the culprit. Another reason for caution is the possible inclination to focus on changes over time and to ignore continuities as insignificant. Quite often it is the very lack of change that is the more important feature of the analysis. For example, an analysis of fertility trends before and after the arrival of the contraceptive pill in the early 1960s suggests that the pill had no significant impact on fertility rates. This is just as important sociologically as if there had been a sudden reduction in the birth rate.

- *To make comparisons between groups* - these could be used to illustrate some aspect of a group's situation or lifestyle and maybe as phenomena to be explained (eg gender patterns in admission to prison or mental hospital).

Official statistics as topics

A controversial, if technical, example of this would be to explore the official definitions of poverty and low income and the way they are selected and presented in official statistics. The coverage they receive from the media or information from unofficial sources, like pressure groups, could be used as well, such as to assess the reaction to the government's figures.

Generally this would be an obscure debate, but it became highly topical and political in 1989 when the government changed the way it estimated the number of people on low incomes, as defined by below half of average income. Johnson and Webb, from the *Institute of Fiscal Studies,* an independent research body, analysed the different impact these changes in calculating the numbers on low income had on the estimates made. The new method reduced the number counting as being on low income by 1,130,000 (Johnson and Webb 1989/90).

Other commentators at the time noted other relevant changes in government statistical practice, including the abolition of the *Royal Commission on the Distribution of Income and Wealth*, changes in the method of counting unemployment and so on.

Another controversial issue can be used to illustrate the source/topic, witting/unwitting distinction. Official criminal statistics can be used as a source, even if problematic, but they can also be studied as topics or data in their own right. For example, twice in the early 1980s the Metropolitan Police or the Home Office released figures about crime in London which included a statistical breakdown of the victim's impression of the offender's race. However, only robberies and other violent thefts (just 3% of recorded crime) were selected for this treatment. Indications were that over half the offenders were black. The reports made no comment on whether or not the victims' impressions were seen as reliable. Neither did they make reference to the racial identities of other crimes, such as insider share dealing, football hooliganism or serious breaches of factory legislation. Furthermore, the high profile given to black people as offenders, however selective the crimes involved, contrasts sharply with the low profile given to black people as victims, notably of racial abuse and violence (see Abercrombie et al 1988, page 261). As Martin Kettle said in the *Sunday Times* (27-3-83), 'The presentation of these figures tells us more about the people who released them and about the people who wrote them up than about crime in Britain.'

It may be difficult to imagine doing an enquiry wholly on bias or racism in official statistics but the idea that these data are worthy of study and comment, in their own right is an important one.

Representativeness, reliability and validity

The evaluation of statistical, and other, data rests heavily on the application of three key concepts: representativeness; reliability; validity (McNeill 1990).

Firstly, and briefly, representativeness. This is a central issue where the research covers only part of the population which the sociologist is interested in (such as sample surveys). The ability to generalise, with confidence, from the smaller group to the whole population may depend on the former being typical of the whole group. As we have noted in passing, the government carries out a number of sample surveys and there are times when representativeness could be an issue in evaluating the data so gathered. In general terms it is safe to assume that the Office for Population Censuses and Surveys, for example, does seek to obtain appropriate representativeness in the sample surveys with which they are concerned. However, that can become difficult if there is a relatively low response rate, such as with the *Family Expenditure Survey* (ie 30%), and where these respondents may come from one social group rather than others.

The concepts of reliability and validity are more complex. Reliability refers to the extent to which repetition of the research by someone else, or the same person later, produces the same or, at least, consistent results - assuming, of course, that the phenomenon being measured, for example a set of attitudes, has not changed.

ACTIVITY 6 - ASSESSING RELIABILITY AND VALIDITY

1 Estimates of the Resident Population

The estimates of the resident population are based on figures from the latest Census up-dated to allow for births, deaths and migrations into and out of the country. They include residents temporarily outside the country and exclude foreign visitors. Members of HM and foreign armed forces stationed here are included, but members of HM armed forces stationed abroad are not (Source Key Data *1987).*

a. Does the above explanation seem a valid definition of the resident population? (Remember it is not attempting to measure the British population.)
b. In terms of reliability, how would you assess the following components of the population measure used above:

1 census data?   3 migration figures?
2 birth and death rates?   4 armed forces stationed here?

Slattery (1986) gives a very useful discussion of some of these sources.

2 School or College Attendance Registers

a. How reliable are they as measures of attendance?
b. How valid are they as measures of institutional involvement in the school or college?
c. What other measures might be used to assess involvement?

NB All these questions relate to the issue of operationalising concepts, discussed on pages 98-99

Generally, if a research technique is reliable, it is also thought to be accurate. The concept of validity goes further and asks whether or not the method measures what its users claim it to be measuring. Thus, 'If an item is unreliable, then it must also lack validity, but a reliable item is not necessarily also valid. It could produce the same or similar responses on all occasions but not be measuring what it's supposed to measure' (Bell 1987).

This is all rather abstract; let's take some examples to illustrate these points.

• *Divorce* - Given that the only way of getting a divorce in Britain is through official channels - the courts - then there will always be a record. Leaving aside divorces abroad, the divorce figures are therefore highly reliable. Someone may still have added up the numbers wrongly of course. The big question with divorce figures, however, is what they actually mean. Because there were so many barriers to divorce in the past, it is often argued that rises in the divorce rate cannot simply be taken as a measure of marital breakdown. However, we are not suggesting that changes in the divorce rate in the last three decades or so can be explained without reference to changes in rates of marital breakdown.

Suicide - Jack Douglas' phenomenological critique of Durkheim's use of official statistics can be used to illustrate a second issue of validity (usefully discussed in Douglas 1967). One of his main points was that we need to take account of the variable moral meanings or social definitions of suicide. He was not just referring to the important explanatory issue here that, for example, a person who considers a suicide a sin is presumably less likely to take her or his own life than someone who has no such moral scruples or definition. There is the separate issue of whether a person who commits suicide believing it to be a sin is actually engaging in a comparable act, say, to someone who kills himself in the pursuit of honour (World War 2 Kami Kazi pilot?). From the physiological point of view, the result is the same, but does it make sense to count them as if they were sociologically identical?

The point can also be illustrated by reference to divorce. Its legal definition, if not grounds, is the same now as in the 1930s but socially and culturally it is quite different. This brief comment highlights the contrasting ways the ideal typical sociologist and lawyer differ in their approach to the same subject (see sections on sociological perspective, pages 8-9, 16-20, 44-47 and see Berger 1966, pages 40-41).

Before leaving this section, we need to pick up on a comment on page 69 about *Britain 1990 - An Official Handbook*. Whilst recognising the professional reputation for independence that the British Civil Service and its statisticians have, we do need to retain a sceptical approach to all official versions of events. This is what Berger (1966) called the 'debunking motif in the sociological consciousness...' leading sociologists 'to unmask the pretensions and the propaganda by which men cloak their actions with each other'.

We have already noted the possibility that government figures on low income are calculated with political impression management in mind; there are many such examples that can be sought out, depending on your chosen topic. Concern about government manipulation of official statistics has often focused on the twenty or so changes in the way unemployment is counted, introduced over the last ten years (see Slattery 1986). Of more general interest, however, are the comments from Muriel Nissel, editor of *Social Trends* 1970-74. In an article in the *Guardian* (15-2-90) she argues that there have been 'subtle' changes to this publication in the last ten years, so that the circumstances of the low income groups in society are given less prominence in criteria for selection and presentation, as are other data showing the government's or the nation's performance in a more critical light.

It is for these reasons that you should always try to look for critiques or alternative sources of data on the topic in question.

CHECKLIST - STATISTICAL SOURCES

 Are you intimidated, mathematically or by fear of positivism (!), from using statistics? If so, please think again.

 Have you considered the wide **range** of agencies, institutions and organisations that may be useful sources of statistical data for your enquiry? These could be local, national, international; official or unofficial.

 Have you explored the various **ways** that statistics from secondary sources can be of assistance to you in your enquiry, either as a major focus or source or as one small source among many?

 More especially, have you looked at the many ways secondary statistics can be important **sources of data** as the main content (particularly on topics where primary research is difficult); as background for your enquiry; as a basis for checking and comparing your own findings and so on?

 Alternatively, have you considered using a set of statistics as a **topic of study** in its own right, looking at the process by which statistics are constructed, assumptions made and so on?

Have you given sufficient attention to the analysis and evaluation of these data in terms of **representativeness, reliability, validity and bias**?

6

Documents

For the purposes of your sociological enquiry, you could usefully define a document as any material - written or pictorial - which provides you with data for your research. This is a deliberately broad definition but we would stress that we are not including here sources that are covered elsewhere: media, statistics or books. We are including reports, both official and unofficial; minutes, memos and records from organisations; publicity material; political leaflets; signs in shop windows etc. In other words, the range of material that counts as a document is so wide because we are including material that its producers intended to be used as a source of information, say a government enquiry, as well as a wide range of other material which you have to convert into sociology by the way you use it.

This distinction is in line with the witting\unwitting use of sources discussed in the introduction to Part II. These two approaches are illustrated at several stages below. Before looking more fully at types or sources of documents, a couple of points need to be made that stem particularly from this unwitting use of documents.

Firstly, whereas the number of sources or types of documents that can be used in a witting sense is large, the range and number that can be used in the unwitting sense is immense. This means that it is impossible to provide an exhaustive list of documentary sources or types.

Secondly, whilst it is usually quite clear how a document can be used as resource for the information it contains and is intended to convey, the use of documents in the unwitting sense is not so obvious. This means that a list of types or sources of documents without explaining how or why they are sociological sources would be of limited value. Because, therefore, a complete list of sources is impossible and a list of sources without comment on their usage is undesirable, we have outlined some general document types with some discussion of their possible uses as we go along.

Finally, in this introduction, we should like to emphasise the importance of analysing documents using the important evaluative concepts of reliability, validity and representativeness as discussed in the chapter on statistics (pages 73-75). One particular point could be made on this. Where you are using documents as a resource for information about society, bias should be noted but seen as a weakness in the data. Where you are analysing documents as topics in their own right, bias is part of what you are studying and is in no sense a weakness in the data.

Types and uses of documents

Reports and commissions
These are probably the types of documents that most readily spring to mind as sources of socio-

logical data. Many are likely to be government sponsored or financed; others will be from pressure groups, churches, charities and other voluntary associations. A good example of a government report is the Swann Report (1985) on the education of ethnic minority school children. Clearly this could be used as a resource to obtain information and ideas on the topic of race and education. Another example would be *Domestic Violence: an overview of the literature* (1989); as its title suggests this HMSO publication pulls together much of the available research on this topic. Government reports should not, of course, be treated as gospel. We need to ask who was on the inquiry team or committee, what its terms of reference were and crucially, where possible, find other information on the report, such as media criticism or data from non-governmental organisations. In evaluating government reports, you might note the view of many commentators that there has been a general shift in the nature of government reports and commissions. They argue that, for much of the post-war period, a characteristic form of government inquiry was the Royal Commission or similar body; examples from the 1960s would include the Plowden Report (1967) on *Children and their Primary Schools* and the Donovan Report (1968) on *Trade Unions and Employers' Associations*. One of the chief features of such commissions was that its members represented a cross section of major institutions and views across the party political divide although radical opinions of the right or left were usually excluded. There would be academics, trade unionists, capitalists (managers or entrepreneurs), representatives of voluntary organisations, the churches, the professions and so on. This can

be seen to reflect what has become known as the period of consensus politics.

Since the 1979 General Election, there seems to have been a move away from this type of inquiry to one based on a narrower range of members and viewpoints. This is part of Mrs Thatcher's rejection of consensus politics in favour of 'new right' solutions to problems. Take, for example, the 1985 reviews into the biggest shake up of social security since the 1940s. The four committees had a total of eighteen members, of whom a half were government ministers, allowing for the fact that some ministers were on more than one committee. There were four representatives from private companies (biscuits, electronics, two from insurance) and at least three representatives from right wing organisations (Institute of Directors, Adam Smith Institute). There were no trade unionists or representatives of the leading poverty organisations. In addition to this, there has arguably been another political change which has affected the nature of the organisations you may be seeking documentary information from. This concerns those organisations set up and (partially) funded by government, sometimes called Quasi Non-Governmental Organisations or QUANGOS for short. One writer comments:

'In 1979, a Government was returned to power which determined to exercise much greater control over QUANGOS. Many of them, especially those incorporated by the royal charter, enjoyed a protected autonomy. However, by increasing the number of members, replacing retiring members and vice-chairmen by politically acceptable nominees, by hiring and firing senior executives it was possible for the government to exercise control. Other QUAN-GOs besides the Sports Council suffered in this way including the Manpower Services Commission, the British Broadcasting Corporation and the Arts Council.' (McIntosh 1987, p 119)

It is hard for you to assess these changes without knowing more about the documents or organisations that concern you, but it reminds you of the value of obtaining as much background information on your sources as you can and the importance of using a range of sources of data, not just the one.

It isn't only government reports which have been accused of bias. The editor of the *Sunday Telegraph*, Peregrine Worsthorne, accused organisations like the *Child Poverty Action Group* and *Shelter* of sounding like 'extensions of the Labour Party' and of being 'unreliable' (*Sunday Telegraph* 18 December 1988). Interestingly, in 1989, there was a major controversy over a report published by *Shelter* based on research on young people in - or rather outside - the housing market. *Shelter* asked 100 homeless youngsters to fill in diaries on a daily basis giving details of their lifestyles and circumstances. For this they were given £5. The survey results, which were quite dramatic in the extent of reported suffering, were featured in a television documentary and *The Observer* newspaper. The *Sunday Times* claimed that the diaries were fabricated, that they were politically biased and that this had put the Department of the Environment grant and *Shelter*'s charitable status at risk.

This allegation was vehemently denied by *Shelter*, including by a Conservative MP on its board (Robin Squire, Hornchurch). *Shelter* ar-gued that the *Sunday Times* report contained large elements of fabrication, that the journalist concerned had largely written the story out of pique because he had wanted exclusive coverage for his own newspaper. *Shelter* have reported him to the National Union of Journalists, the Ethics Council and to the Press Council for abuse of media privilege.

Again, the key lesson to be learned from this is that sources should always be evaluated critically, even if, or rather, especially if you agree with them.

So far this discussion has focused on using documents as resources for information. A good example of the unwitting use of documents is provided by Solomos' analysis of the assumptions and stereotypes underlying government reports on black youth from the 1960s onwards (Solomos 1988). In particular he points to the way in which official reports tended to define black youth in terms of two stereotypes: the idea of black youth as a time-bomb waiting to revolt; and the social and cultural deprivation image, associated with ideas of insufficient assimilation of so-called British values and culture, negative assumptions of British family life and so on. He also looked at ways in which policy based on these assumptions could well have reinforced, or even produced the situations they claimed to describe. In other words, Solomos related his analysis of documents to information gained from other sources - a very useful and common practice.

Another illustration, taken from a different area, is Wilson's (1977) exploration of the sexist assumptions that have regularly informed and shaped official thinking on social policy. A classic example comes from the most important social policy document of the twentieth century - The

Documents

Beveridge Report (1942) where one section states:

'In the next thirty years housewives as mothers have vital work to do ensuring the adequate continuance of the British Race and of British Ideals in the world.'

You are not going to undertake research on anything like the scale of these two writers but some analysis of a relevant report along these or similar lines should be possible, as below for example.

A student of ours read reports on alcoholism from various agencies, such as Alcoholics Anonymous (AA) and Drugs, Alcohol and Women Nationally (DAWN). She contrasted the image of alcoholism and alcoholics and related them to what she saw as the semi-religious orientation of AA and the feminism of DAWN.

Records

Many organisations keep written records on their members, clients, patients and so on. Examples are medical social work reports, housing authority files, court reports and so on. Access to these is a major problem for sociologists although professional researchers are sometimes given or gain access. Thus in the 1960s Aaron Cicourel spent several years doing participant observation research in California as an unpaid probation officer. Shipman (1988) points to the way Cicourel, an influential phenomenologist, used the documents:

'To Cicourel each report must be treated as a particular interpretation within a general situation. His book, *The Social Organisation of Juvenile Justice*, uses records, but not as a source of information on delinquents, but to show how they come to be defined as delinquent.'

Closer to home, Richard Skellington analysed comments on file, by local authority officials in Bedford, finding many of them to contain quite racist comments (*New Society*, 29 January 1981).

From your point of view such access is impossible. However, there are reports which could be available and used to good effect. You might consider school or college reports as a source of data, for example. Other students, relatives, friends etc may be prepared to let you study theirs.

Clearly the report is intended to inform the pupil and her or his parents about that pupil's record, behaviour and so on (its witting content). What else might you be able to tell from a report (the unwitting evidence)? Make a list, bearing in mind ideas about the curriculum, hidden curriculum, assumptions about gender, race or class, images of the model pupil etc.

If you do research of this kind you will have to bear in mind the representativeness of your sample and not make unsupportable claims.

Minutes and memos

Minutes are the written record of a meeting, whether it be a sports club, school governors' meeting or Cabinet Committee. Memos are the internal notes and communications that are sent between staff and members of an organisation; copies of these are often kept on file. Overall it is much more likely that you will be able to make use of and have access to minutes than memos but, as we shall see, there are occasions when memos can be extremely valuable to the sociological researcher.

Minutes of a meeting can be brief and highly bureaucratic: secretary's report - agreed; correspondence noted etc. This certainly does not communicate much in the witting sense and possibly very little in the unwitting sense either. Alternatively, some sets of minutes can be informative in the sense that they tell you how issues actually get on the agenda for discussion; what was said or agreed, if anything; any action that was recommended etc.

In interpreting sets of minutes you need to take note of the fact that minutes are only condensed versions of the proceedings, written from a particular perception of those proceedings. It may be that the minutes have to be approved by someone in authority before they are written up. In this sense, they may tell us quite a lot about what those in power want their members or staff to know.

This last point reminds us that some minutes are for internal consumption only and outsiders to the organisation or committee will generally have no access to them. Personal involvement and/or contacts can be useful here but beware of the ethical and legal issues of confidentiality and trust.

Depending on your choice of enquiry, it would certainly be worth while exploring access to minutes of local council meetings; contact your local town hall on this. Councils often discuss issues of considerable significance - school closures, equal opportunities policies, policing etc - and can provide useful data for your enquiry. Your local paper often covers these meetings or lists forthcoming committees; it's worth a look through its columns to find out what issues are currently being dealt with by the council.

At a grander level, there are the minutes of all debates in the Houses of Parliament, known as Hansard. These are available at larger public libraries. Like minutes of council meetings, Hansard can be extremely valuable to the sociological researcher. In both cases it is important to remember that it is not simply what politicians are trying to tell you that is important but what ideas of society, what belief systems seem to be behind their arguments.

Parliament may discuss poverty, race relations, abortion, crime, housing, drugs, standards in broadcasting, one parent families, attitudes to other societies and so on. The way these issues are defined in debates in Parliament can be a valid part of a sociological study, particularly since these definitions are amongst the most influential in society.

One well known sociologist whose work involved this kind of analysis was Stan Cohen (1972). He was interested in a wide range of reactions to the bank holiday events in several seaside resorts in 1964, as part of his research into moral panics and mods and rockers and, as part of this, looked at comment made by magistrates, MPs in the House and so on. Another example of the sociological use of parliamentary comment and debate is provided by one of our former students. He analysed the speeches made during a law and order debate in Parliament on 'short, sharp shock' policies in the early 1980s. He then tried to link sociological theories of crime to the suggested explanations of ministers and opposition MPs.

Court reports can be equally valuable, particularly the summing-up or sentencing speech of the judge. Judges seem to have a habit of making extremely sexist comments about rape, rape victims and rapists and these are often reported in the press. Whilst they can be used as evidence of judicial attitudes, you need to be careful about generalising from a sample that is small and possibly unrepresentative. It isn't just rape and it isn't just crime that judges make pronouncements upon however; their criminal and civil judgements cover race relations, tax and social security fraud, trade unionism, peace protesters and so on.

Finally, before leaving this section, we repeat and emphasise that you can be alerted to many of these proceedings by keeping an eye on the media. This obviously includes the press but TV programmes like *World in Action* and *Panorama* can be very useful also. Indeed the media sometimes publish leaked memos or minutes that you would not otherwise have access to. Sometimes leaks are made deliberately by civil servants who are disillusioned or want to expose what they see as immoral government policies. At the other extreme, there are leaks which are deliberately made by government ministers or press officers as a way of spreading rumour or misinformation, to discredit opponents for example. Whatever the reason, leaks are highly selective and cannot be trusted to occur at the time you want or to be necessarily any more reliable than information made public officially.

Promotional material

College prospectuses, political manifestos, brochures from pressure groups, packaging on commodities, billboard advertisement, careers leaflets, publicity handouts from societies and organisations, literature from neighbourhood watch groups - all these are examples of promotional literature.

In different ways, they can be invaluable sources of data to the student researcher. They may be used as evidence, as in the way assumptions about gender are sometimes indicated by packaging on toys; or they may be used simply to illustrate an idea, as in Edmund Leach's use of the cornflake box in his discussion of 'the cereal packet norm' idea of the nuclear family.

In this, as in other documentary sources, the witting/unwitting distinction is crucial. Take a school or college prospectus, for example. It can be used as a source of information, as a resource in its own right. It might tell the reader the size of the school, the curriculum on offer, the number of computers or laboratories and so on. It will, however, contain other information which its authors did not directly intend to convey or did so only incidentally. The gender of the headteacher or principal may be indicated and a sample of prospectuses may be used for research into male dominance in educational institutions.

Clearly, promotional material, by its very nature, is biased; its contents are consciously selected and presented to promote a particular impression. In some respects this is 'tarnished' information. But where the research is directly focusing on the way images are promoted or presented, then that bias in the prospectus becomes direct evidence in its own right.

Sometimes bias will be unconscious, as in the way some attitudes, such as sexist ones, can be deeply embedded in a set of taken-for-granted assumptions. Sexism may be indicated in the words and pictures of a college prospectus, without its producers being aware of it. Of course you need, as always, to be cautious in your interpretation of this data. It is better to use 'seems to indicate' than 'prove' when the certainty, interpretation or weight of evidence is in doubt, as it often is.

A good example of publicity or promotional material comes from a GCSE student of ours, who was doing an enquiry on adoption. A leaflet from the British Association for Fostering and Adoption designed for intending adopters was a useful source of data. She did not use it for its description of adopting procedures but to see if she could discover what images of family life were being conveyed: middle class? white? single or two-parents? desired numbers of children? In short, what ideology of the family was presented in addition to the factual material of the leaflet?

Another student researching abortion, having received information from the pro-abortion group, National Abortion Campaign, and the anti-abortion group, Society for the Protection of the Unborn Child, began by seeing what she could suggest about these organisations simply from the quantity and expense of material that was sent without charge.

We hope these examples give you some indication of the wide range of uses you can make of what might at first appear to be irrelevant blurb of a non-sociological kind.

Clearly pressure groups, commercial organisations and political parties are amongst the most obvious sources of promotional literature and you can, of course, write to these organisations. Other material may come along by chance: a poster in the street, some 'junk-mail' through the letter box for example. This can't be planned for and its availability depends on a combination of chance, alertness and sociological imagination.

Concluding remarks

The discussion in this chapter referred back to some general issues of data use and evaluation, such as reliability and validity. It also looked at some specific examples of various types of document, indicating problems of interpretation and so on. In conclusion we refer to Scott's recent and useful discussion of documents in social research (1990).

Firstly, we should note that, in his definition of documents, he includes reference books, official statistics, and the press, sources which we have discussed separately to give more commentary and guidance. Nonetheless, it does mean that Scott's valuable observations are not just relevant to this particular chapter of the book.

Secondly, his article is a general discussion of documents rather than a guide to their usage. Because of this, he raises some issues which the Sociology A level student researcher may not need to go into - such as historical problems of authenticity perhaps (see below).

Thirdly, his discussion inevitably overlaps with observations of ours, both in this chapter and elsewhere in the book, even if the terminology differs. Nonetheless, because his is such a clear guide to general problems of interpreting documents, we provide here a rather full summary of his main points.

Whether it be a set of minutes from a boardroom conference or a pupil's school report (our examples), Scott argues that any document should be assessed according to four criteria: authenticity; credibility; representativeness; and meaning.

By authenticity, he is referring to whether or not a document is complete and reliable (soundness), eg no pages missing and in terms of whether the author is who it is claimed to be (authorship).

Credibility concerns whether or not the author of the document believed what she or he had written to be true (sincerity), as well as if it

---

Criteria for evaluating documents

AUTHENTICITY:
> Soundness and
> authorship

CREDIBILITY:
> Sincerity and
> accuracy

REPRESENTATIVENESS:
> Survival and
> availability

MEANING:
> Literal and
> interpretative
> understanding

Source: Scott 1990

The question of representativeness is partly about the fact that the social researcher may only have access to a limited number of documents, either because of secrecy (availability) or loss over the passage of time (survival). If there are only a few documents available, how much weight should be placed on them? There is the reverse problem when the number of documents available is enormous and here Scott rightly argues that: 'The sampling of documents must be handled as carefully and systematically as the sampling of respondents in a survey.'

The fourth issue is that of meaning. This partly relates to the surface interpretation of the document (literal meaning) or what we refer to as witting usage. Scott points out that this interpretation is not always simple, for example, because some documents are in old or difficult-to-translate languages. It also relates to a deeper and (interpretative) understanding of the document, our unwitting usage. Here he contrasts the quantitative approaches of content analysis with the qualitative analysis known as semiotics, associated with media or cultural analysis.

actually was true (accuracy). For example, some government statements may be written with sincerity yet be inaccurate because of innocent error, ignorance or whatever. However, there are other times when government documents may be written or leaked (see page 82) with the intention of misleading its readers.

CHECKLIST - DOCUMENTS

 Have you considered all the organisations or agencies that consciously produce documents related to your enquiry topic and whether or not these are available, either on general publication or on request?

 Are there documents of any other kind that could provide evidence or illustration of an aspect of your research topic? There are obviously no systematic lists here; the only guidance is to be alert and imaginative.

 Are the documents you have discovered best used as **sources** of data or as data in their own right, to be analysed as **topics**?

 What meaning and weight have you accorded to the document?

 How do the concepts of **witting** and **unwitting** usage, **reliability, representativeness** and **validity** apply to your use of the document? (Alternatively Scott's overlapping but slightly different criteria for evaluating documents could be useful: **authenticity, credibility, representativeness** and **meaning.**)

Are any of your documents directly or indirectly discussed elsewhere such as in the media or in academic literature? If so, have you used this as a possible source of evaluating the documents?

7

Observation

What's observation good for?

The observer is often a romantic figure in sociology. You will probably have come across the work of researchers whose studies lead them into exotic underworlds of drugtaking, delinquency or madness (eg Young 1971, Patrick 1973, Goffman 1968b). You may have an impression of the observer as an undercover agent, even a voyeur, a loner who is not afraid of the seedy, the dangerous and the unknown. By contrast other methods - analysing official documents or standing in the rain with a clipboard - may seem tame and less glamorous.

Observation does not have to be of exotic or bohemian lifestyles and cultures. Of course, there are good reasons why it may be an appropriate method for the study of groups which are on the fringes of respectability - 'outsiders' in Becker's terms. But, it's just as likely that you will use more mundane forms of observation in your study.

You might attend a meeting of a group whose activities are related to your enquiry, a residents' Crimewatch committee meeting, a public meeting held by Friends of the Earth or perhaps a local council meeting.

You might spend some hours observing some aspect of institutional life - teacher/pupil interaction in the classroom, gender differentiated play behaviour, interactions between customers and shop assistants and so on.

Alternatively you could make some small aspect of public behaviour the focus of your study; the sociology of queueing, behaviour in lifts, or on the beach are possible examples, although there are many others. Such minor and taken-for-granted aspects of daily life are interesting and appropriate territories for student enquiry. If you're interested in this sort of observationally based study, you will find some useful examples and conceptual starting points in the work of Goffman (1971). His life-as-drama ('dramaturgical') approach is particularly appropriate to the micro-sociological analysis of everyday life.

Varieties of observation

From these examples, it's clear that observation can vary considerably. There are two main dimensions to the types of observation possible. One is the degree to which the observer joins and becomes part of the group or setting being studied. At one extreme, there is participant observation where the researcher becomes a member of the group and is involved in their activities and at the other extreme the observer remains outside the group, not joining in at all. The second dimension is the degree to which the researcher reveals to those being studied that s/he is doing research (see box on page 87).

In reality research can never be as neatly categorised as this. The distinctions we have made

VARIETIES OF OBSERVATION

	Observation	Participant Observation
Overt	Researcher not involved in group but makes no attempt to conceal fact of observation. eg observing effectiveness of different teaching material in classroom use.	Researcher joins setting as participant but doesn't hide the fact that s/he is observing. eg observer working behind the counter of a 'fast food' chain observing how staff define and interpret 'customer relations' training.
Covert	Researcher observes situation from 'outside' and does not reveal to group that they are being studied. eg observing the effect of a patient's dress and demeanour on their treatment by hospital receptionist staff.	Researcher becomes a normal participant in the setting and conceals the fact that research is being done. eg study of how a group of male and female teenagers describe to their peers their experiences of 'dating'.

above are not either/or options. For example, there are degrees of 'overtness'; you may be more open with some of those you're studying than others (eg Whyte's (1955) special relationship with 'Doc') or you may proclaim a role which is partly true (eg Corrigan (1979) described himself to the school children he was studying as a 'cockney writer'). In our experience, students have often found it was sufficient to say they were 'doing a project'.

The boundaries between different types of observation are also blurred by the fact that the observer role is likely to change during the research period.

Despite these reservations, the two dimen

sional model does highlight some of the problems of different observational styles:

- Non-participant observers, as outsiders, may have difficulty getting to grips with how the individuals they are observing define reality.
- Participants face the problem of objectivity, there is a danger, even for the experienced sociologist, of over-involvement with the group, often referred to as 'going native'. Participant observers can also find themselves having to play a part in situations they find morally unacceptable or which are illegal.
- Overt observers can find the knowledge that they are being observed may influence the behaviour of the group they are studying.

- Covert researchers face the ethical dilemmas raised by their deception of the group being observed.

Observing everyday life

Because they are so familiar, the rules that govern everyday behaviour are often difficult to detect. As accomplished social actors they seem to us to be natural, obvious and just common sense. Garfinkel (1967) suggests that one way we can bring the taken-for-granted aspects of reality to the surface is consciously to break these rules. He once recommended his students to examine taken-for-granted rules of family life and relationships by behaving as though they were lodgers in their own homes. To the consternation of parents and other family members, these students offered rent, asked permission to use the sitting room, addressed those they had known all their life with formal politeness and so on. This brought the expectations that family members have of each other into much sharper focus. It also, incidentally, caused a good deal of disturbance and distress in family relations - 'Why are you treating me like this?', 'Why don't you behave like a proper son/daughter?' etc.

Such reactions raise more ethical issues. You should bear the possible effects in mind if you attempt strategies of this kind. Remember that you have responsibilities to those you are studying, and to other student sociologists whose own research may be made more difficult by the public impression of sociology as a discipline that you help to create.

We began this chapter with the question: 'What's observation good for?' We have suggested that observation can be used in student enquiries in a number of ways. These may vary from the brief 'snapshot' observation of a passing event or situation to a more extended ethnography of a particular group or activity where observation forms the central methodology. Even if observation is not your main method, the following discussion should help you make the best use of observational information.

Getting into the situation

Obtaining access to a group or activity for the purposes of observation can be difficult. However, settings which are normally open to the public pose few problems for the observer. In some cases it may be advisable to make a formal approach. If, for example, you wish to observe some aspect of public behaviour in a shopping precinct or a railway station, permission from the management is advisable. At least you will avoid being questioned by security staff on suspicion of shoplifting which happened to one of our students carrying out research in a department store. Generally it's best to get permission for observation so that you're covered if something goes wrong. Do consult with your tutor when you're planning observational activities and get advice on the best approach strategy.

Access can be more difficult where you're planning to observe in more informal contexts, for instance a club, an occupational group or a subculture. Problems of access should be considered at the earliest stages of the project. In our experience, enquiries of this sort are most likely to be successful if you have already established some contacts with the group concerned.

Access can be very time consuming; developing relationships with people, gaining their confidence and so on all take time. Certainly we would advise that you carry out some sort of feasibility study at the planning stage to avoid your project being wrecked by access problems later on. Remember that locating a suitable group for observation, and gaining their confidence and acceptance is time consuming and can be disappointing. In general, given the constraints of the student enquiry, we would recommend that you only select groups for this form of study where you are already, to some extent, an 'insider'. However, although prior involvement with a situation may make access easier it may also be harder to be objective about that situation. Even in the work of professional ethnographers, there is an element of chance in finding access to a group. This means that you should be ready to take up opportunities which you did not anticipate.

Your role as observer

In many of the best known observational studies (eg Whyte 1955, Goffman 1968b, Humphreys 1970) the observer's role has been crucial. The success of these has depended on finding an appropriate role within the group. Goffman's investigation of behaviour in a mental hospital owed much of its success to the fact that his role as assistant to the physical education instructor allowed him into the situation but in a role that was outside of the medical staff/inmate relationship. From this vantage point he had access to both inmate and staff groups but was not directly identified with either. Similarly Humphreys' study of homosexual encounters in public toilets was facilitated by the fact he was able to take up the role of lookout which enabled him to observe without becoming a participant.

We do **not** recommend the above studies as models for student enquiries. Undercover observation raises ethical issues concerning the rights of those being observed. In general we would support Polsky's (1967) argument that researchers have a moral obligation to be open about their role and would advise student researchers to proceed accordingly. Again, if such issues arise in the planning of an observation, seek advice from your tutor.

Both studies do, however, show the value of considering carefully your role within the setting you are observing and the opportunities it offers for observing interaction. These are issues which you should discuss in your log and reflect upon in the report itself.

What you can and can't see

A careful consideration of your role within the setting should also heighten your awareness of what you can and can't see as an observer. The nature of Humphreys' covert observation strategy made it impossible for him to find out information about the social circumstances of the men who came to the toilet for sex. The secretive and anonymous nature of this kind of sexual encounter meant that any attempt to pry into the identity of the men was taboo.

Humphreys used the highly suspect strategy of tracing some of the men through their car registration numbers and collecting information about them under the cover of another survey being carried out by the university where he was working. Humphreys has been criticised both for the further deception involved and the risks of police detection his subjects were exposed to by his methods. Leaving aside these important ethical concerns, this does illustrate the need in almost any such study for non-observational data to contextualise the findings. Observation will only provide information which is available to someone playing your role within that setting. Pryce (1979) underlines this point in his comment on the restriction placed on what he was able to find out as someone in a male role: '...as a male researcher I had only limited access to the women in the West Indian community for research purposes...To correct the masculine bias of the research, then, what is needed is a female researcher investigating issues that involve the West Indian female population per se.'

You may, like Pryce, be unable to rectify the shortcomings in your study. It is important that you demonstrate that you are aware of bias, omissions, and the limitations of your role as observer. You should try, where possible, to find alternative sources of information and you should examine these issues fully in your report.

Gathering data

The importance of focus

One of the merits often claimed for observation is its openness. It is a method that is said to be sensitive and receptive to the subjects it studies. During the progress of an observational study, the focus of the study can change and grow as new information and attitudes come to light. Thus there is a kind of natural, organic growth to the study. Some lines of enquiry which the researcher thought promising may wither away and die, while new and unexpected paths open up as the research proceeds. At the early stages researchers are recommended to keep an open mind and to concentrate on absorbing as much of the situation as possible. Polsky expresses this succinctly:

'Initially, keep your eyes and ears open, but keep your mouth shut' (quoted in McNeill 1990).

This is not to say that you can or should approach observation with a completely open mind; whatever their claim, no researcher can ever do this. All perception is filtered through the ideas, attitudes, expectations and assumptions. Examine the surroundings in which you are now reading this book. Make a mental note of the most important features. Now try to describe the same environment as it might be described by an architect, a painter, or a five year old. Each time, different features become prominent, new perspectives on the same scene emerge. In Shipman's words:

'Between the impression of the senses and the reported interpretation are the attitudes, values and prejudices, as well as the academic conceptual models, of the researcher. Perception is the process of fitting what is seen or heard into these maps and frameworks in the mind.' (Shipman 1988)

These remarks are a preamble to the main point we wish to make here that you should approach any observation with a clear focus in mind. This focus will have been developed in your reading around the subject and in the original construction of the research aims. Certainly, subsequent revelations may force you to change tack but you should begin with a clear idea of your destination. We make this point so emphatically because, if you don't have a clear focus, you will have no criterion for deciding which features of the situation to include and which to leave out.

To take a familiar example, suppose you are observing a class. Are you more interested in what the teacher is doing or the students? Is it the formal content or the 'hidden curriculum' that is more important? Is the teaching strategy relevant? Is it worth noting the layout, the seating plan or the facilities and resources available? Should you be recording interactions between students or the language that's being used?

Without a clear focus for your observation, such a list of questions could be extended almost indefinitely. Clearly you could only attend to a few of the features at the same time. But if your focus is sharp (see the classroom observation exercise in the box on page 94) then you will have a much clearer idea of what features of the situation are worth recording.

Despite these remarks, participant observation remains a more open ended research strategy than other methods. It is common for the research focus to shift, sometimes in quite unexpected ways. The flexibility of participant observation and its sensitivity to how individuals define and interpret the world around them is one of its main strengths.

It is essential, especially given the time constraints of the student enquiry, that you start participant observation with a clear set of concepts and issues in mind although, true to the inductive spirit of the method, this may not be where you end your enquiry.

The production of a worthwhile participant observation study involves more than simply 'telling a story' however interesting that may be. To qualify as sociological, it must involve analysis, and that requires the use of concepts, theories and perspectives.

Thorough preparation is most important if your contact with the setting is likely to be only brief - the observation of a meeting for example. The same is true if it's a situation that's difficult to repeat - a student of ours who made a study of kibbutz workers in Israel during her summer break (see page 99) had to be certain that all relevant data was collected while she was there because there would be no opportunity for a follow-up.

The issue of objectivity

We've already raised this problem, particularly in relation to participant observation. There are no easy solutions here, but the following suggestions may help you:

- the discipline of keeping **regular records** of your observation helps to distance you from the situation and gives you some space in which to reflect on what happened. It also trains you to keep your attention on your aims;

- keep up **regular discussion** of the work in progress with your tutor and fellow students. This will help you focus on the relevant sociological issues and generate new ideas and interpretations. A regular reporting back session during class time can be helpful here.

Recording qualitative data

As you are planning the focus of your observation you should, at the same time, develop the methods that you will use to record that data. This section is concerned with qualitative data - descriptive information that cannot be expressed in numerical form.

In many observational settings it would be disruptive to record your impressions immediately. But you should still adopt a systematic approach to the recording of information. This will most probably be in the form of field notes; a carefully structured record of your observations which is regularly updated. Because memory is unreliable, it's vital to write down your thoughts and observations as soon as possible. Thus, your field notes should be written up on the same day as your observation or, if this is not possible, the following morning. Your enquiry log is probably the best place to record such information and you should get into the routine of regular entries.

In certain circumstances video or audio tape recordings are useful because these techniques allow you to postpone the analysis of the interaction. It is also possible to 'replay' sequences for more minute analysis. This method should be used cautiously however for the following reasons:

- Video or audio tape recordings are selective. Aspects of the interaction will be lost if you don't analyse a 'live' interaction.

- Analysis can be very time-consuming. Transcription of the verbal content of a tape will require, on average, ten hours for every hour of recorded material.
- The presence of recording machinery can be intrusive, and inhibit the interaction.

Whether you use live or recorded action, clearly, what you record will depend very much on the focus of your study. Remarks made by participants, actions, even drawings of the positions of actors, may be relevant. Make a note also of what you see as the significance of observations that you record, how they relate to the sociological concepts, theories and hypotheses. The field notes are a record of what you observed and an ongoing account of the development of your ideas. While

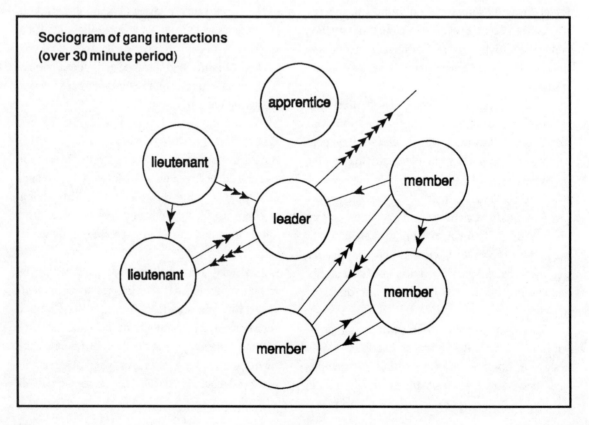

Sociogram of gang interactions (over 30 minute period)

they're primarily an aid to your memory, they also will be a vital reference for you when you come to write up your final report.

Recording quantitative data

Despite the fact that observation is primarily thought of as a qualitative method, some forms of measurement may well be appropriate. There are various ways of measuring interaction processes and you will probably have to choose or develop one which suits the needs of your enquiry focus. The following exercises and examples may help you to make your choice.

Sociograms

This is a graphic representation of some aspect of interaction. Each individual is represented by a circle and the interaction between them represented by linking lines. A mature student of ours observed teenagers at a youth centre where she worked part time. One group of males seemed to be organised into a gang with a clear hierarchy.

There were, she observed, four levels to this hierarchy: leader, lieutenant, member and apprentice. Her quantitative observations, recorded in the form of sociograms, seemed to confirm her impressions of structure.

She observed the group on several occasions for periods of about thirty minutes while they were playing table football or hanging around on the steps of the club. The sociogram was used to record the frequency and direction of interaction. A connecting line showed a communication between two individuals and an arrow indicated the direction of the communication. Further communications were shown by additional arrows. Lines which seemed to point off the page were comments addressed to the group as a whole. A copy of one of her sociograms is on page 92.

Clearly this form of quantitative analysis can only capture limited aspects of social interaction. The samples of behaviour observed were quite small and may not have been representative. Also, the technique concentrates on the process of in-

SCHEDULE FOR RECORDING INTERACTION CATEGORIES				
	Female child	Wife	Male	Husband child
Primary viewing (full attention)				
Secondary viewing (shared attention)				
Tertiary viewing (occasional attention)				

Observation

teraction rather than its content - no record was kept of what was said. There were also some difficulties in classifying interaction into categories, deciding, for example, to whom a remark was addressed or dealing with several remarks spoken at the same time.

Despite these limitations (the student discussed these in her report) sociogram analysis did support her impressions of group structure and showed how these were reflected in group interaction. For example, the leader appeared the most likely to address the group as a whole, and interaction was most frequent between members at the same level in the hierarchy. There are other conclusions which you will probably be able to draw from the evidence yourselves.

If you use some form of sociogram analysis, do be prepared to experiment with it first as prac-

---

ACTIVITY 7 - RECORDING OBSERVATIONAL DATA

Measuring TV viewing styles

Look again at the chart for recording interaction categories which is shown on page 93 for recording different types of viewing. Imagine that you have produced some results for these categories as a result of a series of structured observations and that you are now about to write up your report.

1. Make a list of the points that you would consider in evaluating your data

A useful reference for such research would be Morley (1986) **Family Television**

Gender relations in the classroom

You are engaged in research into gender differences in classroom interaction. From your initial survey of the literature you have come up with the following ideas (hypotheses) which you would like to assess in your own research:

        a. boys are addressed more frequently by name than girls
        b. boys make more demands on teachers than girls
        c. boys occupy more physical space in the classroom
        d. boys interrupt and belittle girls in classroom talk

The school has agreed that you can observe six lessons.

1. Design a research strategy which will provide you with both qualitative and quantitative observational data on these issues. This should include record sheets and instructions for the observer.
2. What role would you adopt in the classroom while doing your observation?
3. What would you tell the teachers and the class of what you were doing?

A useful reference here would be Mahoney (1985) **Schools for the Boys**

tice is essential; do make sure that you show clearly in your report what can legitimately be inferred from such findings.

Interaction categories

With this technique the researcher defines a set of categories into which interaction can be classified. These categories will depend on your research focus - the particular issue that you're interested in studying. They will be influenced also by the sociological concepts and theories you use. Categories should also be based on your prior observation of the setting. This technique is like content analysis where similar problems of categorisation occur (see pages 58-63).

A study of TV soap opera audiences by one of our students illustrates the method. She observed six different families, keeping a record of the type of viewing activity of each family member as they watched a particular soap. The chart on page 93, based upon Tunstall's (1983) classification of media audiences, was used to record results.

In this design, the student made a record of the category of viewing behaviour at five minute intervals during the programme. A tick was placed in the appropriate category for each family member to show their typical viewing style during the previous five minutes.

CHECKLIST - OBSERVATION

 Is some form of observation appropriate to your enquiry (**overt** or **covert**, **participant** or **non-participant**) even if it's not the main source of information on your topic?

 Are you aware of the **strengths** and **weaknesses** of your chosen observation style and technique? Have you addressed these in the development of the research design and in your report?

 What problems of **access** (if any) are involved in doing our observation - how were they overcome?

 Have you reflected on the **observational role** you've adopted and considered both what it has enabled you to see and prevented you from seeing?

 Is your method of **recording** observational data appropriate to your aims and the setting?

What means of **evaluating** your data are available (eg by comparison with other research, published statistics and so on)?

8

Questionnaires and interviews

'If you want an answer, ask a question.'
(Shipman 1988)

Those who study human behaviour have a unique advantage over other scientists. The natural scientist studying a galaxy or an atom can observe, measure and sometimes experiment, but only the social scientist can ask questions of their subjects. As we shall see, this further source of information brings both new opportunities and new problems. Anyone can ask questions; the sociological skill lies in asking the right questions and making sense of the answers you get.

Of all the instruments in the sociological toolbox, questionnaires and interviews are probably the best known. These are the two main formats within which sociologists ask questions. The key difference is how the questions are presented; interviewers conduct their questioning face-to-face with the respondent while in the questionnaire the individual responds to questions that are written on a form.

There is an obvious payoff between questionnaires and interviews in terms of **breadth versus depth.** The relative convenience of a questionnaire means that it is a good format for asking the same simple questions to a lot of people. The strength of the interview, although it is more time-consuming, is that it is possible to explore issues in more depth and respond flexibly to the answers.

Defining the problem

Before you decide which is more appropriate for your purposes it is important that you are clear about what you want to find out. Our experience is that student researchers can get into serious problems if they do not have a clear focus. We have already made this point with respect to observation but it applies even more strongly here. If your aims are not clearly worked out you have no guide as to which questions are worth asking.

For example, Goldthorpe et al (1969) approached their study of affluent workers with a specific hypothesis in mind. This arose out of their critical review of prior studies of worker attitudes. In particular, they set out to test the hypothesis of *embourgeoisement*; the notion that workers were acquiring middle class attitudes to work and the home. If it existed as described by previous writers it would be found amongst the Luton sample: well-paid manual workers who were living away from traditional working class communities. This group were typical, therefore, not of the working class as a whole but represented the direction in which working class employment and communities were allegedly moving. Goldthorpe and Lockwood's clear definition of the problem allowed them to identify the population which they were interested in and gave them the basis for the sorts of questions they had to ask.

Questionnaires and interviews

Defining the problem for your enquiry is not an easy task, but you will find that, where there is an existing literature on the subject, this will help you formulate your aims and hypotheses. Not all research, whether by professional or student sociologists, will have a clear hypothesis. Sometimes your initial reading will only suggest a number of general lines of enquiry to pursue. But, if you haven't thought the problem through sufficiently, you won't know who to ask or what to ask them.

Scope and scale

One of the difficulties of defining the problem is keeping your enquiry to manageable proportions. Given the limited resources and time available to the student sociologist, you will have to take some hard decisions about which issues you can tackle and which are beyond the scope of your enquiry.

McNeill (1990) outlines some of the issues in his discussion of an imaginary study of the impact of a new motorway on the surrounding area.

'Who do we ask? Everyone who lives in the area? Including children aged four or five? Should we include people who have moved away because of the motorway? If so, how can we identify and trace them? Perhaps we should include people who work in the area but do not live there? Should we not include people who regularly travel through the area by car, who must have an opinion about the difference it has made to their journey? And what about the local shopkeepers, or owners of cafés and petrol stations? Should they not be investigated as a special category of people affected? How big an area are we going to investigate? Will we not have to make a decision in advance of what the extent of the motorway's influence has been?' (page 19)

It's clear from the above that you have to make a number of decisions which limit the scope of your enquiry - but this is the sort of compromise that any research must make. In small scale student research the limitations of time and money will be quite severe - do not get disheartened by this, it's in the nature of any research. You will, however, get credit for justifying your choice in terms of what's practical and commenting on how your findings might have been affected by the parameters you set yourself.

Operationalising concepts

Once you have defined the sociological issues you wish to address from your survey of existing literature and decided on the scope and scale of your enquiry, the next step is the practical application of the sociological concepts and ideas that you have identified as relevant. This task is known as the operationalisation of concepts. Translating concepts into questions is not easy and it puts your understanding of those concepts to the test. For example, even the widely used category of social class is not easy to apply or operationalise. Do you ask people if they are 'middle' or 'working class'? Do these categories mean the same thing to everyone? Do sociologists agree on their meaning? Is the social class of a child that of its father (by occupation?) or mother or both? And so on.

You might operationalise concepts as one of our students did by rephrasing various alternative sociological theories about delinquency into everyday language in his study of teachers' views of the causes of school misbehaviour. These brief summaries were presented to teachers on cards during an interview and they were asked to comment on them.

We have already referred (page 91) to another student of ours who decided to make a study of the treatment of Israeli kibbutz workers. She had arranged to work on a kibbutz during her summer holiday. Before she left, she had informal discussions with several people who had been before. Some of these had complained of being treated differently from the permanent workers and of being exploited. She followed up some studies of migrant workers - particularly European *gästarbeiters* ('guest workers') – which suggested an interesting comparison between temporary kibbutz workers and migrant workers elsewhere. This gave her the framework for a set of interviews which were conducted while working on the kibbutz. At the same time she was able to carry out some participant observation during her stay.

The sociological concepts of alienation and exploitation were central to this enquiry. Sociologists have different definitions of these concepts (further complicated by the Marxist claim that people may be objectively exploited even though subjectively they are unaware of this condition).

Questionnaire or interview?

The choice between these two formats for asking questions is easier once you know what your focus is, the scale of your enquiry and how you're going to operationalise the central sociological concepts. Each format has its own strengths and weaknesses in particular situations. Again, it is important to show that you have thought about the issues involved, chosen carefully and appropriately, and are able to reflect on the quality of the findings you produce.

Questionnaires, whether distributed by hand or by post, give you quick access to a lot of people but some respondents may not take them seriously and you have no opportunity to correct misunderstandings or give additional prompts. Because you are able to address a standard set of questions to a larger sample of people than you could interview, the results you obtain may be fairly reliable.

But the data you obtain cannot be judged by quantity alone. For instance, the discovery from questionnaire responses that x% of a sample agree with the statement that 'homosexuality is morally unacceptable' is of limited use without knowing how or why they find it unacceptable. In short, do not be persuaded to use the question-

---

ACTIVITY 8 - OPERATIONALISING CONCEPTS

Suppose that you were carrying out the Israeli kibbutz volunteer study described on this page.

Take the Marxist concepts of alienation and exploitation and devise some questions which could be asked of kibbutz volunteers to discover the extent of their exploitation and alienation.

You should consider and try to assess both the subjective (as it is experienced) and objective (as it really is) dimensions of these concepts.

naire simply because it offers the opportunity to survey large groups if the data you gather lacks validity, because you are unsure what people meant when they gave that answer.

Interviews, by contrast, usually have a better response rate - people are more likely to agree to answer questions put directly. On the other hand, they introduce a further variable - your presence as an individual - which can have unexpected effects. Your appearance, dress, age, gender and speech may all affect the answers you get. Furthermore, it is all too easy, even with the most formal and rigid interview format, to unwittingly cue the respondent to give certain answers by nods, smiles or even how you record the response.

To some extent this problem is built into any method that relies on answers to questions. People may offer the answer that they believe you wish to hear, or the answer which they feel is more socially acceptable rather than express what they are really feeling. This effect is stronger in interviews where you are physically present. The skill of asking interview questions is to avoid cueing answers by your choice of words or by your responses and to be sensitive to your influence as questioner. Many of these problems can be ironed out in preliminary questioning and the piloting of questions before the study begins in earnest (see box on page 105).

You should also be aware that, however willing the respondent is to give 'honest' answers, there can be a gap between what people do and what they say. Social psychologists put this clearly when they say that an attitude has three components:

- cognitive - concerned with knowledge;
- affective - concerned with feelings;
- behavioural - concerned with what people actually do.

The contradictions between these three are most apparent when the topic is personal or controversial.

The shortcomings of interviews or questionnaires need not be a handicap to a good enquiry. You can give breadth to an enquiry involving a limited number of interviews by relating your findings to larger surveys carried out by sociologists, government or other agencies. Similarly, you can give greater depth to questionnaire findings by relating them to other more qualitative or observational research. In some circumstances it may be feasible to use two complementary techniques of primary research yourself. As elsewhere, your assessment of the evidence is as important as the evidence itself.

Sampling

Whether you choose questionnaires or interviews, choosing who to ask will depend very much on the nature and scale of your study. In some student enquiries it will be feasible to question every member of the target group. Several past students of ours have carried out enquiries concerned with an aspect of their workplaces (shops, restaurants and so on). In small scale studies such as these it may be possible to question everyone involved. If you can, you will be able to generalise about the group without the fear that your remarks may only be true of those members you spoke to.

But unless the target group being studied is very small, it's unusual for student researchers to study everyone. This is partly a question of availability - you may not be able to contact everyone. More often it's a matter of resources - approaching the whole group would be far too expensive and time consuming. In any case, questioning the whole of the target population is not necessary, because a sample, carefully chosen, can give a representative view of the whole group.

There are standard procedures for selecting samples developed by sociological researchers. **Random samples** are drawn by picking names randomly from a list which is known as the **sampling frame.** For instance, in a study of how pupils choose subjects, you might decide to question a group of third year pupils who are making GCSE choices. A convenient sampling frame for this purpose would be a list of names of all third year pupils; the school would probably provide you with one without too much difficulty. If there are 100 third year pupils and you want a one in ten random sample you could take every tenth name on your list. Professional researchers will use random number tables to select a sample from a sampling frame but the above method would probably be adequate for most student enquiries.

But suppose your preliminary reading had shown that gender was an important dimension in subject choice? A sample of ten, drawn in this way, could easily have two boys and eight girls, even if there are exactly fifty boys and fifty girls in the third year. Another method which would represent these two groups more accurately is **stratified sampling.** In our example, you would need to separate the third years into two lists; one of boys and one of girls, and then take every tenth name from each list. This would ensure that you had appropriate numbers of each gender in your sample. Note that the success of this method may depend on you being able to separate the group into boys and girls on name alone which may be difficult - is 'Pat Smith' male or female?

Stratified sampling becomes even more complex if you want to represent other characteristics (ethnic group, social class etc) in your sample. **Quota sampling** may be the simplest solution. Here you decide beforehand the numbers of each group that you want represented, and then select respondents until you have filled each category.

All sampling is a compromise between representativeness and practicality. Given the limitations on student enquiries, you will often have to make do with samples that are not fully representative. Often practical issues such as the availability of people for interview may influence your choice of who to approach. The most important requirement is that you give thought to the selection of respondents, that you are aware of any sources of bias in your sampling and that you report fully on these in the analysis of your findings.

Designing a questionnaire

Length
Keep questionnaires brief, ten minutes is a reasonable time for completion. If they are long, or take ages to complete, respondents may be put off. Only ask for information which you really need.

Presentation
A questionnaire should be attractively laid out and simple to follow and complete.
- Leave plenty of space around questions; don't cram them together.
- Place any response boxes in a column down the right hand side of the page.
- If you are going to code answers for later analysis (see recording responses pages 107 and 109) leave space for this too.

Questionnaires and interviews

If you offer respondents the opportunity to answer in their own words, leave a reasonably sized and clearly marked space for this too.

Instructions

Indicate **how long** the questionnaire will take to complete. State clearly a **return date** (eg please return by Friday 10th October). Two weeks is about the right length of time to allow for the return of a questionnaire; do make sure you take this into account when you put together your plan of action (page 27).

State clearly **how** the questionnaire is to be returned to you. If it's a survey of college students you could ask teaching staff to help with the administration and collection, or you could provide a central and accessible collection point. If the confidentiality of responses is an issue, you must consider the security of completed questionnaires. Answers to questions on student views of staff teaching styles could be influenced by the knowledge that completed questionnaires might be read by the staff concerned. You will also need to take account of the context in which the questionnaire is completed when you assess your findings. How might responses be affected by the presence of others who are tackling the same form?

A poor response rate is a common problem with the questionnaire format. Don't rely on respondents finding you to return forms. Make the procedure for returning them as simple as you can.

Questionnaires that are to be returned by post should be accompanied by a stamped addressed envelope. Take care with this method as postal costs can soon mount up. To send and return 100 questionnaires by first class post currently costs

£44 in postage alone; photocopying a two-page questionnaire might add a further £20, unless you have free access to a photocopier.

Preamble

This is a brief statement explaining the purpose of the questionnaire. The success of a questionnaire is dependent on the goodwill of your respondents. You are much more likely to keep this if you make clear what's involved, do not make unreasonable demands and give an assurance of confidentiality.

Like any other professional group, sociologists set themselves ethical standards for their dealings with the public. It's normal practice to give an assurance of confidentiality, and your responsibility for this lasts throughout the research. It involves keeping information securely, not revealing anything given in confidence, and making all reasonable efforts to conceal the identity of the individuals you have studied. This problem arose in a study by one of our students into middle class delinquency. He included a photograph of the group he had interviewed in his report making identification very easy!

There are standard procedures for overcoming these problems. In *Learning to Labour*, Willis (1977) gave false names to the 'lads' whose conversations he quoted extensively and also invented 'Hammertown' as the pseudonym for the city in which he was researching.

The preamble should be clearly printed at the top of the questionnaire or it could be included in an introductory note distributed with the questionnaire.

Sample preamble

'Please would you answer the following questions on the community care of mental patients. Your responses will help in research that I carry out into the care of people with mental disorders for my sociology A level course. I am interested in your personal views which will be treated in confidence. Please do **not** put your name on the questionnaire. The questions should take about ten minutes to answer. The information I gather will be written up in a report which is part of my A level assessment.'

Devising questions

- Make sure each question is **relevant** to your aim/hypothesis.
- **Language** - keep the wording of questions as simple and direct as possible. It's always important to keep in mind the group that you're dealing with and make your questions appropriate to them. This means you must be familiar with the group before you start. Generally avoid long sentences. Do not use technical language or jargon from sociology or elsewhere. State in full the names of organisations (eg Campaign for Real Ale, not CAMRA). Avoid vague words such as 'often', 'many' or 'usually' and so on. It's likely that people will interpret these differently. Do not use language that might be thought of as emotive or offensive by those you're studying.
- Avoid questions that **assume something** about the respondent. Problems can arise if you presume, wrongly, that respondents share knowledge, attitudes or experiences that you have had, particularly as people may not admit their ignorance. Ask yourself whether your respondent can be expected to know the answer.
- **Multiple questions**, which ask a respondent to give a single answer to what are effectively two or more separate questions, can cause confusion. For instance, the interviewee may agree with the first half of the question but not with the second. If this is a closed question, where response categories are predetermined, this problem becomes particularly acute. The best solution is to rephrase into two or more separate questions.
- Answers to **hypothetical questions** are often unreliable, especially if the person being asked has little direct experience of the situation you describe. Generally it's best to avoid them.
- Questions which make **unreasonable demands on the memory** can also cause problems. For example, it's not fair to expect someone to remember which television programmes they watched in the last month or to recall, with accuracy, details of their childhood. In the case of television viewing patterns, you could get more accurate results by asking your subjects to keep a daily viewing diary.
- Take care not to ask **leading questions**. These suggest, in the way that they are worded, that one answer is more popular, more acceptable or preferable in some way.
- Group questions into a **logical sequence**. Thus, questions on related subjects should go together and, reading through the sequence, there should be a natural, conversational flow. Always begin with some easy and non-controversial questions. Issues which are complex, challenging or personal are best approached later. When planning a sequence, write down

ACTIVITY 9 - WHAT'S WRONG WITH THIS QUESTION?

The following list of (invented) questions contains examples of many of the flaws described in the guidance of constructing questions on page 103.
Read this through again and then make a note of the flaws that you have found. Beware, some questions may contain more than one!

1. Do you take regular exercise?

2. Was your first sexual partner:
        a. more experienced than you;
        b. less experienced than you;
        c. about the same?

3. If you had a portable telephone would you use it:
        a. in a public house;
        b. in a restaurant;
        c. on public transport;
        d. at a friend's house?

4. What is your favourite aerobic activity?

5. Should the vicious and degrading spectacle of boxing be banned?

6. Is poor parental discipline responsible for the decline in the behaviour of schoolchildren?

7. Most people believe that ecological issues are not taken seriously enough by politicians. Do you agree?

As a further activity, can you reword the above questions to make them more effective bearing in mind the design issues discussed on page 103?

the questions on cards and then rearrange them until you find the best order.

- Choose **closed questions** where the respondent is offered a selection of predetermined response categories where you are dealing with factual or neutral issues and where you can reasonably anticipate the likely responses. When asking about age, for example, adults may be more comfortable choosing an age range (20-25, 26-30 etc) than baldly stating their precise age. The closed format can also give helpful cues to the type of information that you require. Eg How often do you go into a public house? At least once a week, at least once a month, ... never etc.

- Choose **open ended questions** if you're uncertain about the range of possible responses. Open ended questions produce responses that will take more time to analyse and which may be more ambiguous. Usually it will be necessary to categorise responses into different types.

Pilot study

Although you may be tempted, do not miss out this important stage where you test your questionnaire on a small number of people. It's easy to overlook flaws; a questionnaire may be perfectly clear to you but misunderstood by your respondents. It's much better to discover this at the pilot stage when something can be done about it.

Pilot studies are most effective when carried out on people who are like those you will approach when you begin in earnest. But, if you're pushed for time, the comments of fellow students or relatives are better than nothing. Some questions seem quite reasonable until you attempt to answer them so make sure your respondents attempt the questions rather than just read through them. The box on this page gives some advice on getting feedback from the respondents of your pilot study.

A PILOT STUDY QUESTIONNAIRE

After conducting your pilot study, you should ask your respondent about any difficulties s/he noticed. The following list, suggested by Bell (1987) for piloting questionnaires, is a guide to the sorts of issues you should raise.

    a. How long did it take you to complete?
    b. Were the instructions clear?
    c. Were any of the questions unclear or ambiguous?
    d. If so, will you say which and why?
    e. Did you object to answering any of the questions?
    f. In your opinion, has any major topic been omitted?
    g. Was the layout of the questionnaire clear/attractive?
    h. Any other comments?

You are now ready to produce the final version. You may need to rephrase questions which cause confusion, modify the sequence, add prompts and so on.

Interviews

Types of interview

In considering the relative merits of interviews and questionnaires we have implied that there is just one type of interview. In fact, interviews do vary considerably in format. On the one hand, the **formal interview** has standard questions which the interviewer follows strictly. By contrast, **informal interviews** flow more freely like a normal conversation. Here the interviewer allows the discussion to develop more unpredictably responding to what the interviewee says. Despite this, the interviewer will have a list of themes which will be covered at some point in the course of the interview. Between these two types, a number of hybrid forms are possible, where the degree of formality and interviewee control varies.

The formal interview has a lot in common with the questionnaire format. Thus many of the design issues already discussed in relation to questionnaires apply equally to the design of a formal interview schedule. If you are using formal interviews you should look closely again at this section.

Length

Whichever type of interview you are conducting, it's your responsibility to indicate how long it will take, not to allow the interaction to wander aimlessly and, ultimately, to bring the interview to a

---

THE INTERVIEWER EFFECT

An interviewer can extend, cut short or re-direct what the interviewee says by nods and smiles, shifts in position, holding or relaxing gestures, utterances such as 'umm' and 'yeah' and so on. Our power to control in this way what others say to us is often unacknowledged, but it is still very real. It's illustrated well in the following example:

> Teacher: ...that's how I see it or that's part of my experience too
> Interviewer: Mm
> Teacher: I suppose that there are other things that they understand...that they don't have experience but I don't think that's as easy to notice.
> Interviewer: Mm
> Teacher: It's not as immediate, that comes out later...
> Interviewer: Mm
> Teacher: ...perhaps in written work and discussions...
> Interviewer: Mm
> Teacher: ...later on.

It's difficult to be certain from this short extract of the interview transcript, but the interviewer's 'mm' seems to help the teacher continue and develop the flow of thought.

(interview transcript quoted in Meighan et al 1979)

QUESTIONNAIRE LAYOUT AND CODING

This box illustrates the layout and coding of questionnaires. Below is a modified extract from a questionnaire schedule originally produced by **New Society** magazine in conjunction with the ATSS (Association of Teachers of Social Science); the original contained twenty-one questions. This is a closed questionnaire which has been precoded; each answer has already been assigned a code (1a for a 'female'; 3c for 'fairly satisfied' with your education at school or college etc). Underneath we have devised a summary sheet to demonstrate how you might summarise the results from a large number of respondents.

Questionnaire schedule

1. Sex

Female	____ a
Male	____ b

2. Age

Under 14	____ a
14-16	____ b
17-19	____ c
Over 19	____ d

3. How satisfied are you with the education you are getting at your school or college? Please tick.

Highly Satisfied	____ a
Satisfied	____ b
Fairly satisfied	____ c
Not satisfied	____ d

Summary Sheet Results for 5 Respondents

Code	1(SEX)		2(AGE GROUP)				3(SATISFIED?)			
	a	b	a	b	c	d	a	b	c	d
Person 1										
Person 2										
Person 3										
Person 4										
Person 5										

Enter your data by putting a tick in the relevant box. Adding down the column then gives you totals for each response (eg adding the 2b column gives you the number of subjects who were in the 14-16 age category. If you only need to know the total for each answer then you could have just one large box for each response category (1a, 1b, 2a etc).

But if you wish to cross reference responses to two (or more) questions you must, of course, keep a separate line for each person. Then, by looking down the columns you would be able to read off, for example, how many boys aged over 19 were satisfied with their education at school or college (ie those with a tick in 1b, 2d and 3b)

close. It's difficult to be precise about length in informal interviews, but don't go on until the interviewee loses interest or patience.

Presentation

As we have said, the central difference between questionnaires and interviews is your presence as interviewer. In interviews, the question of presentation becomes one of how you present yourself and how you ask questions. We have already referred to leading questions (page 103) which imply certain answers are preferable or which give away the views of the person asking. In the interview, there is the added danger that you lead the interviewee non-verbally even if the language of the question is not biased. Complete objectivity in interviewing is probably impossible. However, you should be aware of your own views, particularly if they are strongly held, and keep careful control of them during the interview.

One of our students who rang the home of a local councillor, found herself talking to his wife. 'Who are you?' she demanded suspiciously. Our student gave her name and instantly the woman replied: '...a rose by any other name...' and hung up. The point of this story is not to remark on the infidelity of local male councillors!Instead, it illustrates the point that when you conduct an interview, you are seen as a person, a social actor. Motives are attributed to you and, whether you like it or not, assumptions are made about the kind of person you are, your social identity. These may be completely inaccurate, but they are nevertheless important because they form the basis of the way your interviewee responds to you.

Some sociologists (eg Atkinson 1982; Schlegoff 1972) take the detailed analysis of talk (see box on page 106) very seriously. Indeed one

branch of sociology, conversation analysis (itself an offshoot of ethnomethodology), takes the minute, frame-by-frame analysis of verbal interaction and the ways in which meaning is constructed as its main focus. We are not saying that you should attempt to dissect every nuance of your interviews in this way. But if you are going to understand the responses that you receive, you should at least be aware of the existence of such processes.

Introduction

As with the questionnaire, an important aspect of the interview is how you introduce yourself. Always explain who you are and what your enquiry is concerned with (see section on introducing the questionnaire pages 102-103).

There are often formal channels that you should go through when approaching subjects for interview. Get a letter of introduction from your tutor on headed school/college notepaper which explains who you are and what you are trying to do. Second, be flexible about interview arrangements, be prepared to offer alternative dates and times, bearing in mind the work, family and social commitments that people have.

Recording results

Interviews can be recorded in two ways: by taking notes or by using tape recorders. Unless you are very good at shorthand, you will not be able to take verbatim (word perfect) notes of what is said. Several techniques can help you record the interview:

- develop your own shorthand abbreviations;
- use concept trees to record ideas (page 34);
- it may be helpful to use pre-arranged headings to help you structure your notes.

You may prefer to tape record the interview although some interviewees may object to this. If you rely on tape alone, you are really only postponing the problem. A full, verbatim transcription of an hour-long interview will take about ten hours. Probably the best option, if you are going to use a tape recorder, is to take notes as well. After the interview, use the recording to write up your notes, to jog your memory and to clarify ambiguities.

Pilot interviews

As with the questionnaire, a pilot study will help you develop the best method for recording the interview and also allow you to practise other interview skills.

Analysing results

In this section we deal with the results of both interview and questionnaire data.

Coding closed questions

These are most likely to have been used in the questionnaire format, although they could occur in a formal interview. Closed questions have a multiple choice format (see box on page 107). Each response would be given a code, so that when the responses from each individual are recorded you do not have to write out the answers in full. The code for the answer is then transferred to a summary sheet and columns can then be totalled. An alternative is to use a computer database program. The advantage of this method is that you can produce totals and cross-reference categories without having to do any arithmetic yourself. Some programs will also automatically produce graphs, charts and other graphic displays of the information.

Correlations and causes

Interviews and questionnaires are likely to produce correlational data; they may give evidence of a relationship between two variables, eg gender and voting behaviour. Be careful how you interpret any such finding for two reasons. Firstly, how representative is your sample? (see pages 100-101). If it's very small or biased in some way then any correlation you discover may not hold true for the population as a whole. Secondly, you cannot infer a causal relationship from a correlation. If, as some psychologists have argued, there is a correlation between the type of punishment (physical or psychological) received during childhood and the development of conscience, we cannot infer that beating (physical punishment) causes adult immorality or that verbal reprimand (psychological punishment) causes moral behaviour. A correlation simply shows a relationship between variables but not which causes which. In our example it could logically be the case that moral behaviour is inherited and that 'bad' children so infuriate their parents that they resort to spanking!

Drawing conclusions

In general, be cautious in the generalisations that you make. Always take into account how the information was gained, sources of bias in the questioning process and the representativeness of the group studied. You will not be penalised for caution; modest claims with suggestions for the direction of future research are much more likely to be acceptable than grand assertions of sociological truth which cannot be supported by the data!

CHECKLIST - QUESTIONNAIRES AND INTERVIEWS

 Is some form of questionnaire or interview appropriate to your enquiry even if it's not the main source of information on your topic?

 Are you clear about the rationale for selecting a questionnaire or an interview as your research strategy?

 If you are planning a questionnaire or interview, have you a clear idea of your **aims**, **scope**, **scale** and **sample** for your research?

 Are your questions **simple, intelligible, straightforward**; and do they give your respondents an opportunity to express their thoughts adequately? Where relevant, have you checked this with a pilot study?

 If you are conducting an interview, have you thought through whether formal or informal interviewing is more appropriate? Can you justify your choice?

 Have you chosen an appropriate method to record your results?

Have you carried out a **thorough analysis of your findings**, rather than assume that they will 'speak for themselves'? Does this include an evaluation of your findings by comparison with other studies or other data?

Part III

Organisation and presentation

Includes

Putting it all together

9

Putting it all together

The purpose of this chapter is to help you assemble the information you have collected into the written report which forms the main basis of your assessment.

The importance of the report

Although some syllabuses include other elements of written work (eg the scheme for the London Board which reserves 20% of enquiry marks for the diary) the majority of your marks will come from the written report. However thorough your reading and research or however sociologically significant your findings, if you are not able to present your work well in the written report you will not get the credit you deserve.

Nevertheless, it is possible to recover at the report stage from an enquiry that has gone badly by giving a careful analysis of what went wrong and why. On the AEB scheme, for example, two thirds of the marks for method are for the understanding and evaluation of your chosen method and only one third for success of its application.

As we have said before, the examiners do not expect you to produce startling new sociological knowledge, they are more concerned that you know enough sociology to assess what you have been able to find out.

Previous experience of marking enquiries suggests some students believe that projects are assessed by quantity rather than quality. Avoid the temptation to include everything. While examiners are looking for evidence that you have read widely, they are also looking to see that you understand and can apply concepts and that you are able to pick out what is relevant from the rest. Keep within the recommended guidelines for length (not more than 5000 words for the AEB and London A/S) and do not assume that doing more will earn extra marks; you may even be penalised for enquiries that grow to excessive length because of repetition or the inclusion of irrelevant material.

The report format

The written report is not just an extended essay. It is a formal report which should follow certain conventions. For instance, unlike an essay, you should divide your report into chapters or sections. They help the task of writing by providing structure and break the job into more manageable parts. The sections discussed below are those suggested by the AEB syllabus and would probably be suitable for most reports of this nature, but check the particular requirements of the syllabus you are following. We have suggested lengths for each section based on the marks allocated to them by the AEB marking scheme. These are not Board requirements but only a rough guide. You are not obliged to stick rigidly to them, and, if you are following a different board's syllabus, you must look carefully at the assessment criteria for that board.

In terms of your report's style, don't over-use sociological jargon; clear simple English is best. This last point should not be read as a recommendation to avoid all sociological concepts and theories, however! Inevitably, some technical terms will be involved.

There are marks for clarity of presentation, but none for 'artistic merit'. You can certainly include illustrations, photographs, diagrams and other graphics if they are sociologically relevant, but not just for decoration.

RATIONALE (length 100/250 words)

This is a statement of your reasons for choosing the topic. You should refer here, but not in detail, to sociological arguments and theories placing your research in the context of existing research and literature. It's appropriate also to mention personal interests, contacts, experience or concerns which led you to this choice. The rationale should also define the central issues of your research, either in the form of general aims or specific hypotheses. Keep this section brief; it's not the place for an extended discussion of the sociological background which should be in the 'context' section (see below). Its purpose is to demonstrate that you have thought through the implications of your choice of topic. Some of the issues that we raised in Chapter 2 (eg topics involving personal commitment) may be relevant here.

CONTEXT (length 750/1250 words)

This should contain a selective review of related work. It's necessary to keep a firm control here. If your study concerns the educational opportunities of an ethnic group for example, do not rewrite a text book chapter on the sociology of education but choose those elements which are relevant to your research focus. It could involve, in this case, work on the family, stratification or employment. If your topic is not in the sociological mainstream, you should say here what use you have been able to make of related concepts, research and theories. Make sure you have read our advice on using books (see Chapter 3).

METHODOLOGY (length 400/750 words)

Present here the methods of your enquiry, saying how you came to select them. In doing this, it's quite appropriate to talk about approaches which you considered but rejected, giving your reasons. A carefully kept diary will help you here as a reminder of the reasoning behind your choice of method and, in the London Board syllabus, you should cross refer to the log in your discussion. You should also write about the strengths and weaknesses of the methods that you use, whether primary or secondary. We have discussed these much more fully in the relevant sections and you may find it helpful to refer to these. As in the context section, avoid a 'textbook' discussion of methods in general, keep your focus on those which are relevant to your topic. Don't get involved in a detailed assessment of what you were able to find out as this is more appropriate for the 'evaluation' section (see page 118).

CONTENT (length 750/1500 words)

This contains the main body of your findings. The structure of this section will, of course, depend on the nature of your enquiry. You will probably need to introduce some further sub-headings to organise the presentation of material. For example,

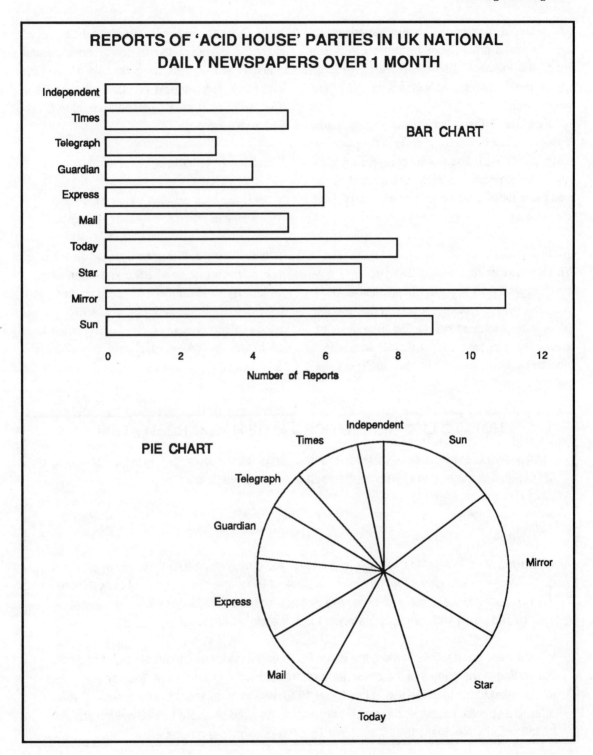

REPORTS OF 'ACID HOUSE' PARTIES IN UK NATIONAL
DAILY NEWSPAPERS OVER 1 MONTH

BAR CHART

PIE CHART

the content section of the enquiry described on page 26 would probably split into three sub-sections; one for each different research strategy (moral panic analysis, subcultural analysis and lyric analysis).

Keep the information in this section fairly descriptive. The evaluation section is the place for analysis, detailed discussion, comparison with other sociological research, theoretical arguments and the evaluation of the success of your methodology.

Qualitative data

Where you refer to evidence that you have collected, support your argument by quotation. What the examiners are looking for here is that you are able to extract relevant information from the mass of data that you have collected. This means that you should never expect the data to 'speak for itself'. Don't, for example, just insert the text of an interview and leave the reader to draw conclusions. If you are quoting the words of your informants, these should be clearly distinguished from the body of your report and placed in quotation marks, eg:

As one 14 year old boy said to me:

'No, the teachers don't care at all about teaching us - they're only after an easy life.'

In line with our earlier comments on the ethics of such research (see page 102), you must disguise the identity of respondents by pseudonyms (false names) for people and places. In exceptional cases, you may cite the words of actual individuals but if you do, you must always check that the individual is willing to be quoted at the time of the

HOW TO LIST REFERENCES - THE HARVARD SYSTEM

This system is easy to use and avoids the addition of messy footnotes. In your alphabetic list of authors referred to in your report each author is cited thus:

(surname)	(initials)	(year published)	(title of book)	(place)	(publisher)
Gwilliam,	P.	(1988)	Basic Statistics,	Harmondsworth:	Penguin

When you want to refer to this book in your text you simply write (Gwilliam 1988) and you don't have to write out the full details of the book. If the same author has published more than one book in the same year these are distinguished as (Gwilliam 1988a), (Gwilliam 1988b) and so on and listed separately in full in the alphabetical list.

Where there are multiple authors these are listed once, under the name of the first author, but adding in the names of the other authors. If there are more than two, the convention for referring to these in the text is (Hall et al 1970) where 'et al' means 'and others'. If you refer to a specific passage, page numbers should be cited. A quote from Gwilliam should be followed by (Gwilliam 1988:73) where 73 is the relevant page number.

GUIDELINES ON PRESENTATION OF THE REPORT.

1. Write only on one side of the paper.

2. Leave a margin so that text is not hidden when the report is bound.

3. Keep the different sections of the report separate starting each on a new page.

4. Number all pages on the final version of your report but not before as amendments will have to be made. If you use a wordprocessor, this is automatic.

5. Include a title page containing: title, your name, your examination number and the centre number.

6. Include a contents page listing the main sections and giving their page numbers (including appendix items).

7. The report can be handwritten, wordprocessed or typed.

8. Hand in the original version not a photocopy (it is, nevertheless, a good precaution to keep a copy for yourself). You can include, however, photocopies of materials that you insert into the text; eg a newspaper article or a pamphlet.

9. Use lightweight binding materials not stiff board ring binders, your enquiry may have to be included in the sample posted to the external moderator.

---

interview or questionnaire and then confirm the actual words with your respondent before including them in your report. In general, we recommend that you go for anonymity.

Quantitative data

As we have already argued, even where the main body of your evidence is qualitative, some quantifiction may be relevant. Try to avoid vague terms such as 'often', or 'several' if you can be more specific. For example, it's better to say that marriage was mentioned by 15 out of 20 girls and 3 out of 20 boys when talking about their future than to use vague terms like 'many' or 'few'. You may of course need to use comparative words when describing data, for example, from a table of statistics, but, wherever possible, avoid vagueness.

Graphics and tables

If you have numerical data it will often be more convenient to summarise these in tables, graphs and charts. Suppose your analysis of national daily papers over a period of a month showed that acid house parties were mentioned by the *Sun* nine times, the *DailyMirror* eleven times, the *Star* seven times, *Today* eight times, the *Daily Mail* five times, the *Daily Express* six times, the *Guardian* three times, the *Daily Telegraph* three times, the *Independent* twice and *The Times* five times.

The box on page 115 shows how this information can be presented in pie chart and bar chart formats. Information presented in this way is more easily compared, analysed and understood than a row of figures.

Pie charts are calculated manually by adding together all the categories (60 in our example) and then calculating the number of degrees of the circle (total 360 degrees) for each category. Thus for the *Sun* the calculation is:

$$\frac{9}{60} \times 360 = 54°$$

Using a protractor mark a segment of 54 degrees starting from the twelve o'clock position. Repeat this operation for all other categories; a calculator will help with the arithmetic.

- Headings should be clear and specific.
- Label categories clearly; if space is limited use colour shading and provide a key.
- If you present your results in a table, keep figures in line vertically.

If you can get access to a computer it will do all the calculations for you. You just enter the data, label the diagram and print a copy. Ask someone in the science, maths or computing department to help you. If you are working manually, use graph paper; it's easier to be accurate.

Sophisticated statistical skills are unlikely to be necessary for student sociological enquiries.

Perhaps the best test of your data-presentation is to show it to someone who is not familiar with your research to check its comprehensibility. For further guidance on descriptive statistics see Gwilliam (1988).

EVALUATION (length 600/1250 words)

The evaluation of your enquiry's findings is an important element of your overall marks. This section should contain your assessment of the information you have been able to gather and a discussion of its strengths and weaknesses. As we mentioned earlier in the chapter, a thorough examination of the work you have done can help you achieve high marks even if the study was flawed or incomplete. Here you should compare your research with that of professional sociologists interested in the same field. Because of the limited scope of student research your conclusions are likely to be in the form of cautious suggestions rather than firm statements. If, however, your study indicates some ideas for subsequent research do mention these.

The evaluation should also include your judgement of the methods of research that you employed. If your study included primary research, interpret the significance of your findings in terms of the sample size, and its representativeness. Mention also any biases which might have affected what you have been able to discover. In short, it's better to show yourself aware of any shortcomings in the study - if you don't, the examiner will be led to conclude that you have not noticed them.

Sources

We recommend that you use the Harvard system for written references, which is the one used in this book. In the system, all references to books, articles etc are marked in the text by the author's surname and the date of publication. Full details of these are then compiled in a list of references arranged alphabetically by author's surname (see box on page 116).

The sources section can include any other relevant data that was not part of the text but which may be required by the reader. Normally this will include the research diary (compulsory

under the London A/S). You may also add an example of the questionnaire if used, audio or video taped material, publicity materials which you have collected and so on. Remember our earlier warning about leaving material to 'speak for itself'. Although you may feel it appropriate to include such information, you will only be assessed on what you have been able to **write** about it in the main body of the report.

CHECKLIST - PUTTING IT ALL TOGETHER

 Is your report in the format required by your examining board and does it include all the required elements: section headings, references, contents page, log and so on (see guidelines box on page 117)?

 Is your research firmly placed in the context of other relevant or related sociological theories, concepts and studies?

 Have you carried out a thorough analysis of your findings whether they are based on primary or secondary sources?

 Will your submitted work stand up as a complete and self-contained report of your research that would make sense to someone who is a sociologically informed reader, but who, unlike your teacher, had no prior knowledge of the enquiry?

 Finally, the most important question, have you satisfied the assessment objectives of your examining board?

References

Abercrombie, N., Warde, A., Soothill, K., Urry, J. and Walby, S. (1988) *Contemporary British Society*. Cambridge: Polity Press.

Atkinson, J. M. (1982) 'Understanding Formality: the categorisation and production of formal interaction.' *British Journal of Sociology*, 33, 1, pp 86-117.

Barrat, D. (1986) *Media Sociology*. London: Tavistock.

Becker, H. (1963) *Outsiders: Studies in the Sociology of Deviance*. New York: Free Press.

Bell, J. (1987) *Doing Your Research Project*. Milton Keynes: Open University Press.

Berger, P. (1966) *Invitation to Sociology*. Harmondsworth: Penguin.

Beveridge Report (1942) HMSO.

Bilton, T., Bonnett, K., Jones, P., Stanworth, M., Sheard, K., and Webster, A. (1981) *Introductory Sociology*. London: Macmillan.

Burgoyne, J. and Clarke, D. (1983) 'Reconstituted Families.' In Rapoport, R. N. et al (eds) (1983) *Families in Britain*. London: Routledge & Kegan Paul.

Carr, E. H. (1964) *What is History?* Harmondsworth: Penguin.

Cashmore, E. (1982) *Black Sportsmen*. London: Routledge & Kegan Paul.

Cohen, S. (1972) *Folk Devils and Moral Panics: The Creation of the Mods and Rockers*. London: MacGibbon & Kee.

Cole, T. (1986) *Whose Welfare?* London: Tavistock.

Corrigan, P. (1979) *Schooling the Smash Street Kids*. London: Macmillan.

Donovan Report (1968) *Royal Commission on Trade Unions and Employers' Associations*. London: HMSO.

Douglas, J. (1967) 'The Moral Meanings of Suicide.' *New Society*: 13-7-1967.

Durkheim, E. (1970) *Suicide*. London: Routledge & Kegan Paul.

Field, F. (1981) *Inequality in Britain*. London: Fontana.

Garfinkel, H. (1967) *Studies in Ethnomethodology*. Englewood Cliffs, N.J.: Prentice-Hall.

Gavron, H. (1966) *The Captive Wife*. London: Routledge & Kegan Paul.

Gerbner, G. et al (1982) 'Programming health portrayals: what viewers see, say, and do.' In Pearl, D. et al (eds) *Television and Social Behaviour: Ten Years of Scientific Progress and Implications for the Eighties*. National Institute of Mental Health.

Glasgow University Media Group (1976) *Bad News*. London: Routledge & Kegan Paul.

References

Goffman, E. (1968a) *Stigma*. Harmondsworth: Penguin.

Goffman, E. (1968b) *Asylums*. Harmondsworth: Penguin.

Goffman, E. (1971) *Relations in Public*. Harmondsworth: Penguin.

Golding, P. and Middleton, S. (1982) *Images of Welfare*. Oxford: Martin Robertson.

Goldthorpe, J., Lockwood, D., Bechhofer, F. and Platt, J. (1969) *The Affluent Worker in the Class Structure*. Cambridge: Cambridge University Press.

Gwilliam, P. (1988) *Basic Statistics*. Harmondsworth: Penguin.

Halsey, A. H. (ed) (1988) *British Social Trends Since 1990*. London: Macmillan.

Hargreaves, D. (1967) *Social Relations in a Secondary School*. London: Routledge & Kegan Paul.

Harker, D. (1980) *One for the Money*. London: Hutchinson.

Harrison, P. (1983) *Inside the Inner City*. Harmondsworth: Penguin.

Hartman, P. and Husband, C. (1974) *Racism and the Mass Media*. London: Davis-Poynter.

HMSO (1989) *Domestic Violence: An Overview of the Literature*.

Hollowell, P. G. (1968) *The Lorry Driver*. London: Routledge & Kegan Paul.

Humphreys, L. (1970) *The Tea Room Trade*. London: Duckworth.

Johnson and Webb (1989/90) cited in *Poverty*, no. 74, 1989/90, Child Poverty Action Group.

Karpf, A. (1988) *Doctoring the Media: The Reporting of Health and Medicine*. London: Routledge.

Kozol, J. (1968) *Death at an Early Age*. Harmondsworth: Penguin.

Lobban, G. (1974) 'Sex Roles in Reading Schemes.' In *Forum - for the discussion of new trends in education*. Spring 1974, vol. 16, no. 2, pp. 57-60.

Mahoney, P. (1985) *Schools for the Boys*. London: Hutchinson

Marwick, A. (1977) *Introduction to History*. Units 3, 4 and 5 of A101, the Arts Foundation Course of the Open University. Milton Keynes: Open University Press.

McIntosh, P. (1987) *Sport in Society*. West London Press.

McNeill, P. (1990) *Research Methods*. London: Routledge.

Meighan, T., Shelton, I. and Marks, T. (1979) *Perspectives on Society*. Middlesex: Thomas Nelson.

Mills, C. W. (1970) *The Sociological Imagination*. Harmondsworth: Penguin.

Morley, D. (1986) *Family Television*. London: Comedia.

Oakley, A. (1976) *Housewife*. Harmondsworth: Pelican.

Pahl, J. (1985) 'Violence Against Women.' In Manning, N. (ed) (1985) *Social Problems and Welfare Ideology*. Aldershot: Gower.

Patrick, J. (1973) *A Glasgow Gang Observed*. London: Eyre Methuen.

Pawson, R. (1989) in Haralambos, M. (ed) (1989) *Developments in Sociology,* Vol 5, Chap 6.

Plowden Report (1967) *Children and their Primary Schools*. London: HMSO.

Polsky, N. (1967) *Hustlers, Beats and Others*. New York: Aldine.

Pryce, K. (1979) *Endless Pressure*. Harmondsworth: Penguin.

Reid, I. (1981) *Social Class Differences in Britain*. Open Books.

Reid, I. and Wormald, J. (1982) *Sex Differences in Britain*. Open Books.

Schlegoff, E. A. (1972) 'Sequencing in Conversational Openings.' In Gumperz, J. and Hymes, D. (eds) *Directions in Sociolinguistics*. New York: Holt, Rinehart & Winston.

Schütz, A. (1971) 'The Stranger', as reproduced in *School and Society*. London: Routledge & Kegan Paul/Open University Press.

Scott, J. (1990) 'Documents in Social Research.' *Social Studies Review*, vol. 6, no. 1.

Shipman, M. (1988) *The Limitations of Social Research*. (Third edition) Harlow: Longman.

Silverman, D. (1986) *Qualitative Methodology and Sociology: Describing the Social World*. Aldershot: Gower.

Slattery, M. (1986) *Official Statistics*. London: Tavistock.

Solomos, J. (1988) 'Institutionalised Racism: Policies of Marginalisation in Education and Training.' In Cohen, P. and Bains, H. (eds) *Multi Racist Britain*. London: Macmillan.

Swann Report (1985) *Education for All: Report of the Committee into the Education of Ethnic Minority Children*. London: HMSO.

Tunstall, J. (1962) *The Fisherman*. London: MacGibbon & Kee.

Tunstall, J. (1983) *The Media in Britain*. London: Constable.

Whyte, W. F. (1955) *Street Corner Society*. Chicago: University of Chicago Press.

Willis, P. (1977) *Learning to Labour*. Farnborough: Saxon House.

Willis, P. (1978) *Profane Culture*. London: Routledge & Kegan Paul.

Wilson, E. (1977) *Women and the Welfare Society*. London: Tavistock.

Young, J. (1971) *The Drugtakers: The Social Meaning of Drug Use*. London: MacGibbon & Kee.

Young, M. and Willmott, P. (1973) *The Symmetrical Family*. London: Routledge & Kegan Paul.

Index